GLOBAL STUDIES SERIES

FOCUS ON

Latin America & Canada

GLOBE FEARON EDUCATIONAL PUBLISHER
A Division of Simon & Schuster
Upper Saddle River, New Jersey

Director of Editorial and Marketing, Secondary Supplementary: Nancy Surridge
Project Editors: Karen Bernhaut and Lynn Kloss
Marketing Manager: Rhonda Anderson
Production Director: Kurt Scherwatzky
Production Editor: Alan Dalgleish
Editorial Development: WestEd, Ink
Art Director: Pat Smythe
Electronic Page Production: Ken Liao
Photo Research: Jenifer Hixson
Interior Design: Margarita Giammanco
Maps and Charts: Mapping Specialists
Cover Design: Marsha Cohen
Cover Art: N. Simakoff

Printed in the United States of America   5 6 7 8 9 10   05 04 03 02 01

ISBN 0-835-91151-9

GLOBE FEARON EDUCATIONAL PUBLISHER
A Division of Simon & Schuster
Upper Saddle River, New Jersey

CONTENTS

MAPS, CHARTS, AND GRAPHS

The World and Its Cultures

Why is it important to learn about the world's cultures?

One aspect of culture is the way people relate to each other. Teenagers in the United States tend to relate to each other in casual ways. What does this tell us about their culture?

Looking at Key Terms

- **culture** the way of life of a group of people, including their ideas, customs, skills, and arts
- **cultural diversity** having a variety of cultures
- **global village** a term that refers to the entire modern world where diverse people communicate, share experiences, and depend on one another for resources
- **extended family** the family unit in most traditional societies, consisting of three or four generations living in one household
- **nuclear family** the family unit in most developed societies, consisting often of a father, mother, and children
- **cultural diffusion** the spread of new ideas and new ways of doing things from one society to others
- **interdependent** the state of being dependent on one another for support or survival

On Assignment...

Formulating Questions: Asking good questions will help you determine the main ideas of subjects you study. As you read this chapter, write questions you would like answered about Latin America and Canada. Look for On Assignment hint boxes to help you formulate your questions. When you are finished reading the chapter, you will finalize your list of questions.

SECTION 1

Focus on Cultures

To what extent does culture determine who we are and how we behave?

- In the United States, people greet one another by shaking hands. In Thailand, people greet one another by bowing low, with their palms pressed together.

- People in some societies, such as the Muslims of Pakistan, do not eat pork. People in other societies, such as the Hindus of India, do not eat beef.

- In some places, such as the United States, people measure wealth by the size of their homes. In other places, such as Papua New Guinea, wealth is measured by the number of pigs a person owns.

A World of Many Cultures

All these differences are differences between **cultures**. Culture is the way of life of a group of people. You may think of culture as what people add to the natural world. All people have a culture.

The people who share a particular culture may or may not live in a single country. For example, people of the Jewish faith live in many countries of the world, including the United States, South Africa, Mexico, and Israel.

One country may contain more than one culture. The United States is a country with people from many different cultures. Therefore, we say that the United States is a country of **cultural diversity**.

The cultural diversity of the United States provides a good reason for us to learn about other parts of the world. By learning about different world cultures, we learn more about ourselves. We learn to appreciate the richness of our heritage.

The World as a Global Village You may have heard people say that the world is becoming a smaller place every day. What they mean is that it is becoming easier to communicate with people around the world. Recent advances in technology have made communication and transportation much easier. As an example, consider the journey of Ferdinand Magellan—the first person to sail completely around the world. In the 1500s, Magellan's journey took three years. Today, airplanes can circle the globe in less than 24 hours. During the American Revolution, it took months for letters from the leaders of the 13 colonies to reach leaders in England. Today, world leaders can communicate instantly by using the telephone, fax, or Internet.

All these changes have created a world that many people refer to as a **global village**. This term refers to the way in which diverse people from around the world communicate, share experiences, and depend on one another for resources.

What Is Culture? When some people think of culture, they think of a symphony orchestra or a dance festival. Culture embraces far more than the arts, however. For instance, if you put on jeans in the morning, listen to rock music, go to school five days a week, and watch football games on television on weekends, you are participating in U.S. culture. On the other hand, if you herd cattle, speak the Setswana language, play soccer, and wear tribal garments, you might be part of the Tswana culture in Botswana.

Culture examines how humans live on earth. It answers such questions as:

- What is family life like in a certain culture?

- How do the people of a certain culture make a living?

- What religions do the people of a certain culture practice?

- What sort of government do they have?
- How does their culture affect the way they interact with the land?

Learning a Culture Culture is learned. However, it is not learned the way you learn algebra or biology. You begin learning your culture the minute you are born. You learn to eat certain foods, wear certain clothes, and speak a certain language. You learn appropriate ways to behave. You learn certain beliefs and customs.

Beliefs and Customs Every culture has specific beliefs and customs. For example, in many Asian cultures, people believe that it is the sons' responsibility to care for their parents as they age. Therefore, families tend to be large. This increases the chance that there will be many sons. Generally, the beliefs and customs of a culture are deeply related to its religion.

Religion Most cultures have religions. Religion is a belief in a superhuman power or powers to be obeyed and worshipped as creators and rulers of the universe. A religion usually includes a set of beliefs and practices that govern behavior. Examples of religions around the world are Christianity, Islam, Judaism, Hinduism, and Buddhism.

Members of a religious group hold similar beliefs about how people should treat one another. They hold similar beliefs about how the world came into existence. Many religious groups believe that there is some kind of life after death.

Language A shared language is one of the most important elements of a culture. Without it, people in a culture would not be able to communicate.

All cultures have languages. These languages express thoughts, beliefs, feelings, and questions. Most people are born with the ability to learn to speak a language. However, the actual language they speak is determined by their culture.

Family Organization In most cultures, the family is the most important unit of life. The family teaches young people how they are expected to behave.

In many cultures, three or four generations of a family live together in a single home or compound. This type of family organization is known as the **extended family**.

In traditional farming societies, a large extended family is necessary to help the family meet its needs. The young and middle-aged men and women of the family farm the land, while older members often look after and teach the children. In other

The nuclear family, such as this one in Thailand, includes a wife, a husband, and their children. Nuclear families can be large or small, depending on the number of children.

In traditional societies, families or villages produce nearly all that they need to survive. In northern Nigeria, villagers trade or sell bowls they have made and goods they have grown.

societies, the extended family is a sign of the culture's respect for its elderly. Families are expected to live with and care for their older members.

In some cultures, the typical family includes a wife, husband, and their children. This organization is known as the **nuclear family**. The nuclear family is common in developed countries. Developed countries have economies based on industry and technology. Families in developed countries often do not need to be large to meet the needs of everyday living. However, a nuclear family is not necessarily small. A nuclear family can have many children.

Economies and Governments

All societies have economic and political systems. Economic systems determine what goods should be produced, how much should be produced, and what the goods are worth. Political systems are ways of organizing government.

Ways of Meeting Economic Needs In traditional societies, families or villages produce nearly all the goods they need to survive. The members of these societies hunt and farm for food. They make their own clothes and build their own homes.

If they produce more than they need, they might trade what is left over for other goods.

In modern societies, individuals tend to specialize in the type of work they do. Because people do not make all that they need, they use money to buy and sell goods and services.

Whether a society is traditional or modern, it has to deal with the scarcity of resources. *Scarcity* means "not enough." In economics, it refers to the availability of natural resources, such as water, or resources made by humans, such as housing. Reasons for scarcity vary. For example, food can be scarce if a region has been hit by drought. Sometimes, one group in society gains power and purposely makes resources scarce for another group.

The economies of many modern societies are organized into free enterprise systems. People are able to start and run almost any business they choose. The governments of such countries make few decisions about what is produced and how much it costs.

Some countries organize their economies in a way called central planning. Here, the government makes almost all of the decisions about what goods are produced and how much they will cost. Governments that use central planning usually own and operate most of the nation's industries.

Most nations today, including the United States, have mixed economies. In a mixed economy, private ownership of business is combined with government control. A mixed economy allows the government to make laws to control the economy and protect the public. Most businesses are owned by individuals and will succeed or fail based on their ability to make a profit.

Government When people live together, they need rules and laws for solving problems. Governments serve this purpose. Governments are made up of people who have the power to create and enforce the rules and laws of society.

There are various ways to organize a government. Below, you will read about three types of governments: democracies, monarchies, and dictatorships.

In a democracy, citizens have the right to participate in government. In many democracies, citizens vote for people to represent them in government. This is the way democracy works in the United States. The main feature of a democracy is that people have the power to shape their government through voting or other means.

In a monarchy, a king or queen heads the government and holds absolute power. Heredity determines who holds the crown. Today, a number of countries have constitutional monarchies. In a constitutional monarchy, the king or queen holds little real power. A body of elected officials, such as a parliament, makes the laws. Britain has such a government.

In a dictatorship, a leader or a group holds power by force. People who express their opposition to the government are usually punished harshly. The country of Iraq is a dictatorship ruled by Saddam Hussein.

Cultures Change Cultures are always changing, although some cultures change faster than others. U.S. culture has changed rapidly in recent years. Other cultures have had few changes in hundreds of years. For example, among the San people of Africa's Kalahari Desert, ways of life have changed little. The San still use simple tools in gathering wild plants and hunting animals.

Cultures borrow items or ideas from other cultures. Blue jeans are an example of this borrowing. Jeans were originally developed in San Francisco in the mid-1800s. These sturdy pants originally were made for gold miners. Less than 100 years later, people all over the globe wear jeans for comfort and for fashion.

Cultural Diffusion The spread of new ideas and new ways of doing things from one society to others is called **cultural diffusion**. The popularity of reggae music is an example of cultural diffusion. Reggae music began in Jamaica. In the 1970s, Bob Marley and other musicians played reggae to audiences in the United States and Europe. The popularity of reggae spread and influenced the rock music of the 1980s, especially in Britain.

A Global System

The world relies on a global economic system. Valuable resources such as oil and iron are not spread evenly. One place might be rich in many resources. Another might be rich in only one. Therefore, the people of the world must trade with one another to meet their needs.

People rely on one another for more than just goods and services. As you read earlier, the world is sometimes called a global village. It can also be said that the people of the world are **interdependent**. *Interdependent* means "people depend on one another." An event on one side of the globe can affect lives on the other side.

With interdependence comes responsibility. Today, conflict between faraway cultures can affect our lives. By understanding other cultures, we can make the differences that separate us count less and the similarities that connect us count more. By cooperating with one another, we can keep our world at peace and in balance.

Section 1 Review

1. What is culture?

2. **Inferring** The United States is often called a multicultural society. The prefix *multi-* means "many." What do you think multicultural means? Why do you think the United States is called a multicultural society?

SECTION 2

Focus on Places

How does a knowledge of geography help in understanding world cultures?

Geography, especially cultural geography, is an important part of global studies. Understanding where people live helps to create an understanding of who they are and why their culture developed as it did.

Two questions geographers ask are:

- Where do people live?
- Why do they live there?

To answer these questions, geographers look at five basic themes—location, place, interaction, movement, and regions.

Location

To study a place, geographers begin by finding out where it is located. A place's location is its position on the earth's surface. Location can be expressed in two ways: absolute location and relative location.

Absolute location is an exact, precise place on the earth. You give an absolute location when you use longitude and latitude. For example, New York City's absolute location is 41° North, 74° West.

Relative location is where a place is in relation to other places. You give a relative location when you say you live 12 miles (19 km) southeast of Columbus, Ohio.

Place

All places on the earth have distinct features that make them unique. Geographers use natural features and cultural features to describe places.

Natural Features When you visit a place, you might notice the sandy beaches, the warm weather, and the tall palm trees. These are natural, or physical, features. Another way to think of natural features is to think of them as the environment.

Take a special look at the environment of places you study because the environment affects how people live. You can identify environment if you look at climate, land, and water.

Climate includes all the elements that make up the weather over a period of time—especially precipitation, temperature, and wind. Climate influences the kinds of crops that grow in a certain region and the type of homes and buildings people make there. It determines the clothing people wear and the types of work people can do.

Land includes the soil, vegetation, mountains, and mineral resources of a region. Land affects crops, animal life, and the work people do.

Water is the third essential part of the environment. Water includes rivers, lakes, and oceans. Water is a vital part of all people's lives. Without it there can be no farming or irrigation. Water can aid transportation and it powers electrical generators.

Cultural Features When you visit a city or country, you might talk about it by describing its delicious food or by describing graceful old buildings that stand by a river. These are cultural features.

Cultural features are the part of the landscape that people add. When you know something about the natural and cultural features of a place, you know what makes it different from other places on earth.

Interaction

The theme of interaction helps geographers understand the relationship between people and their environment.

Every place on earth has advantages and disadvantages for the people who live there. Usually places with many advantages contain large populations. These places are often near water and are flat enough for easy farming. Other advantages might include an

On Assignment...

What would you like to know about the relationship of people and the environment in both Latin America and Canada? Think of questions you would like to ask.

abundance of natural resources that can build an economy.

Fewer people live where it proves more difficult to survive. But people are problem solvers and find ways to interact with their environment. Humans have learned to build aqueducts to bring water to dry areas. They have also carved terraces into mountains so that they can farm the land.

Movement

Geographers use the theme of movement to find out how people, ideas, and products move from place to place.

Many places are made up of people who have moved there from other places. Movement explains why many Vietnamese people live in Texas and California. Some people move because they want to live somewhere with better job opportunities or because they want to escape from a bad situation.

Movement explains the worldwide popularity of blue jeans. Products move when people want something that they do not have. Movement also shows how the religion of Islam spread from the Arabian Peninsula to Africa, Asia, and the United States. Goods and ideas move when people move.

The theme of movement helps you to understand how and why people from one place in the world interact with people from many other areas.

Region

The basic unit of geographic study is the region. A region is a part of the world that has natural or cultural features distinct from

People of all cultures are affected by the environment in which they live. These nomads of southern Jordan have found ways to adapt to the vast desert that is their home.

other regions. The study of regions helps you compare areas of the world. It helps you to see the earth as a system of places that are related in different ways.

You are probably most familiar with political regions. A nation, state, or city is a political region. Regions can be defined by other natural or cultural features. For example, Florida is part of a plains region, a tourist region, and a tropical climate region.

Section 2 Review

1. What are the five themes of geography? How do they help organize the study of geography?
2. **Analyzing** Why is an understanding of geography important in global studies?

SECTION 3

Focus on Change

What changes affect the world's environment?

Geographers and scientists are often called upon to guess the changes that may occur in a region. Predicting these changes helps people plan for the future, avoid catastrophes, and make wise use of resources. One thing geographers and scientists cannot do is stop change from happening.

Some changes result from new inventions and new ways of doing things. For example, fertilizers, pesticides, and farm machines have changed how food is grown. Jets and bullet trains have sped up transportation. Computers have changed how people work and communicate.

Change can be both good and bad. Chemical fertilizers and insecticides improve crop yield but may damage the environments in which birds and fish live. Jets greatly decrease travel time but cause air pollution and noise pollution. Computers and computer-controlled robots make work more efficient but may cause people to lose jobs.

Making Choices

As the world changes, individuals face choices about whether they should support or oppose these changes. They must decide whether to move to cities, use computers, and spray crops with insecticides. You, too, face choices about change. If there are homeless people in your community, you may urge your local government to provide housing for them. If there is air pollution where you live, you may choose to use public transportation instead of traveling by car.

Studying how people of other cultures have changed in both good and bad ways will help you make your own decisions. Learning about other cultures and regions will help you learn about yourself, your own community, and your own culture. You will also discover new things about your relationship to the rest of the world. All of these things are important in preparing you for your role in the global village of the future.

Section 3 Review

1. What are some changes that have had good and bad results?
2. **Predicting** What choices do you think you will make about your community's environment in the future?

On Assignment...

Formulating Questions: Keep a journal of questions you wrote as you read this chapter. When you find facts and examples in this book that answer your questions, write the answers in your journal. If more questions occur to you as you progress through this book, add them to your list.

CHAPTER 1

The Land and People of Latin America

What is unique about the land and the people of Latin America?

Using a canoe carved from a huge tree of the Panamanian rain forest, a woman sets out from the mainland to her home on a island in the Atlantic Ocean.

Looking at Key Terms

- **peninsula** a body of land that is surrounded on three sides by water
- **volcano** a mountain with an opening near the top from which hot melted rocks, ash, and gases sometimes flow
- **tropics** lands that are near the equator
- **moderate** mild
- **mestizos** people who are part Native American and part European

On Assignment. . .

Creating Posters: This chapter covers the land and the people of Latin America. Imagine that you are working for a travel agency to promote tourism in Latin America. Your assignment is to design a poster for an advertising campaign. The theme of the campaign is "Visit Latin America — A Place of Beauty and Diversity." As you read this chapter, look for On Assignment hint boxes. They contain suggestions to help you think of ideas for your poster.

What and Where is Latin America?

What are Latin America's key landforms?

The West Indies separate the Caribbean Sea from the Atlantic Ocean. These islands are actually the tops of an underwater mountain chain.

LATIN AMERICA'S PHYSICAL FEATURES

The Amazon is the second longest river in the world. It runs 3,900 miles (6,275 km). It starts in the Andes Mountains and flows across South America to the Atlantic Ocean.

The Andes is the world's longest mountain range. It stretches more than 4,500 miles (7,240 km) along the entire west coast of South America.

Rio de Janeiro, Brazil, is one of the largest cities in the world. More than 12 million people live there. Cities throughout Latin America are growing at an extremely fast rate.

Latin America is the vast region located south and southeast of the United States. It extends from the northern border of Mexico to the tip of South America, a distance of 7,000 miles (11,200 km). Latin America also includes the islands of the Caribbean Sea.

The climate of Latin America varies greatly. The equator runs through the northern part of South America. That means that Latin America lies partly in the Northern Hemisphere and partly in the Southern Hemisphere. Areas of Latin America around the equator have a hot and steamy climate. Areas near the southern tip of South America are cold throughout the year.

Mountains are one of Latin America's most important landforms. This picture shows Mount Illimani (ee•yah•MAHN•ee), one of the highest mountains in the Andes. The mountain towers over the city of La Paz, Bolivia's largest city. Mount Illimani is part of the Andean mountain range. The Andes is the longest mountain range in the world. It is known as the "backbone" of South America.

The *pampas* are the rich grassy plains of eastern Argentina. The plains of Venezuela and Colombia are called the *llanos* (YAHN•ohs). Ranchers raise huge herds of cattle on the pampas. Farmers grow grains such as wheat and corn. Meat, wool, hides, and grain are the region's most important products. Most of these are exported to other countries through the port of Buenos Aires, capital of Argentina.

The Amazon River, the second longest river on earth, flows for more than 3,900 miles (6,275 km). It sends more water into the Atlantic Ocean than any other river in the world. It rushes through the hot, thick tropical rain forest like a mighty inland sea. The river and its branches are so vast that they drain nearly half of South America.

The Regions of Latin America

Geographers divide Latin America into four regions. These regions are Mexico, Central America, the Caribbean, and South America.

Mexico Of all Latin American countries, Mexico is the furthest north. It is very mountainous, with the mountains running down the middle of the country. On either side of the mountains lie narrow plains. Jutting out on the east coast is the Yucatán (yoo•kuh•TAN) **peninsula**. A peninsula is a body of land surrounded on three sides by water.

Central America Central America is a long ribbon of land that connects Mexico with South America. Mountain chains that begin in Mexico continue through Central America. Many of the mountains in the region are **volcanoes**. A volcano is a mountain with an opening near the top. When a volcano erupts, hot melted rocks, ash, and gases flow from the opening.

A highland area runs through the middle of Central America. Ranchers and farmers in the highland raise cattle and grow coffee and bananas. On either side of the highlands are narrow coastal plains.

The Caribbean The islands of the Caribbean Sea are sometimes known as the West Indies. These islands stretch between North and South America in the shape of a half moon. The largest Caribbean island is Cuba. The smaller islands, such as Bermuda and Anguilla, are only a few square miles in size.

South America South America is by far the largest land area in Latin America. South America contains almost every type of known landform. Its landscape is similar to North America's. Both continents have a high mountain range near their west coast. Both have lower mountain ranges along their east coast. Huge plains with mighty rivers lie in the middle of both continents.

On Assignment...

For your poster you may wish to feature one of the four regions of Latin America. Highlight the natural beauty of the region you choose. Think of words and phrases to describe the region that might appeal to travelers.

Barriers to Movement

The landscape of Latin America has had an important impact on its people. In the past, vast mountains and dense tropical forests isolated people from one another. These natural barriers were very difficult to cross. In recent years, however, modern technology has helped Latin Americans gain a sense of unity. New roads, airplane travel, radio, and television have brought Latin Americans closer together.

Section 1 Review

1. What are the four regions of Latin America?
2. **Analyzing Information** How has Latin America's geography been a barrier to people in different parts of the region?

SECTION 2

The Many Climates of Latin America

What are the climate regions of Latin America?

If you were planning a trip to Latin America, what type of clothing would you take with you? It would not be easy to decide. Here are some of the reasons why:

- From north to south, Latin America stretches over a great distance. This means that some parts of Latin America are near the equator and others are very far away. Most places near the equator are hot.

- Latin America is a mountainous region. A valley close to sea level may be very warm. Meanwhile, only a few miles away, a place in the mountains may be very cold.

- Like any region, Latin America has places where winds blow in different directions. Places where winds blow in from the sea are rainy. Lands near the Amazon River are among the wettest on earth.

- South of the equator, the seasons are opposite to those in North America. Most of South America is located south of the equator. In June, July, and August, when it is summer in the United States, it is winter in most of South America. In December, January, and February, South America has its summer season.

Refer to the map on page 14 as you are reading this section. It will help you understand Latin America's climate regions.

Tropical Climates

About three fourths of Latin America lies in the **tropics.** The tropics are lands that are near the equator. These areas have two types of climates.

In tropical wet climate areas, temperatures are warm, and there is rain throughout the year. Rain falls almost every day, making the air moist and uncomfortable. Look at the climate regions on the map on page 14. What parts of Latin America have tropical wet climates?

The second tropical climate zone in Latin America is called the tropical wet-and-dry climate. This climate is warm throughout the year. However, some months are rainy and some months are dry. Look at the map on page 14. What parts of Latin America have tropical wet-and-dry climates?

Moderate Climates

North and south of the tropical areas lie areas that have **moderate** climates. The word *moderate* means "mild."

The most widespread of these moderate climates is the humid-subtropical climate. Many Latin Americans live in areas with this climate. Here winters are mild and summers are warm. The pampas of Uruguay lie in the humid subtropics.

The Impact of Rain and Wind

Winds and ocean currents also affect climate. In much of the Southern Hemisphere, winds blow from east to west. Winds from the Atlantic Ocean are warm and moist. As these winds move westward, they bring rain to the West Indies and to the northern part of South America.

The winds continue across South America until they reach the east side of the Andes Mountains. There the winds are forced upward. The air is cooled and the rain falls on the eastern side of the mountains. When the air passes to the western side of the mountains, it is dry. Therefore, the area on the west coast has little rain. Here lies the Atacama Desert of southern Peru and northern Chile. In some parts of the Atacama, rainfall has never been recorded.

Vertical Climate

The main influence on climate in Latin America is altitude, or distance above sea level. Within a single country, the climate can vary enormously, depending on whether you are in the lowlands or the highlands. This effect is known as a vertical climate. *Vertical* means "up and down."

At sea level, the climate is tropical, or hot. As you climb into the mountains, the climate becomes somewhat cooler. Near the peaks of the mountains, it is very cold.

LATIN AMERICA'S CLIMATES

Legend:

Symbol	Climate	Description
	Tropical wet (rain forest)	hot, humid, rainy
	Tropical wet-and-dry (savanna)	hot, wet summers; warm, dry winters
	Steppe	hot summers; mild to cold winters
	Desert	hot and dry
	Mediterranean	hot, dry summers; mild, moist winters
	Humid subtropical	hot, humid summers; mild, moist winters
	Marine	warm summers; cool winters
	Vertical	temperature and rainfall depend on altitude

Location and Region Latin America is a land of many climate zones. Is the tropical wet climate zone located near the equator or further away? Why is the vertical climate zone found on the western coast of South America and not on the eastern coast?

On Assignment. . .

A second idea for your poster is to highlight the climates of Latin America. To attract tourists from the Northern Hemisphere, you might point out that during the Northern Hemisphere's winter, it is summer in the Southern Hemisphere.

Section 2 Review

1. Describe two climates found in Latin America.

2. **Making Inferences** Why might someone from Chicago want to travel to the Southern Hemisphere in January?

In January it is summer in Southern Hemisphere.

Winds lose their moisture by the time they reach Salta in western Argentina. The result is a semi-desert similar to the southwestern United States.

SECTION 3

The People of Latin America

What types of people live in Latin America?

Who is an American? When we use that term in the United States, we usually mean people who are citizens of our country. But the people of Latin America are just as American as we are. They live on the continents of North or South America or on islands nearby.

Where Latin Americans Live

More than 460 million people live in Latin America today. Latin America has almost twice as many people as the United States.

It is also more than twice the size of the United States.

Most Latin Americans live in two general areas. One area is the coastal plains. The plains lie on the east and west coasts of the continent. The second area is the highlands. More than 150 million people live in this strip of land that stretches from the Amazon River to the grasslands of Argentina.

The population of Latin America is growing quickly in certain places. Countries such as Mexico, Jamaica, and Guatemala have fast-growing populations. Sudden population increases put a great strain on the economies of these countries. You will read more about the effect of population growth on Latin America's economy in Chapter 5.

A Blending of People

Latin America has a rich mix of people. The people of Latin America fall into four main groups. These are Native Americans, people with African backgrounds, people with European ancestors, and people whose background is a mix of Native American, African, and European cultures. This last group is the fastest growing group.

New Immigrants

Other immigrant groups have also come to Latin America. During the late 1800s, many Asians settled in Latin America. Today, many Japanese make their homes in southern Brazil. Chinese live in Mexico, Peru, and Cuba. On some Caribbean islands, Indians from Asia make up about half the population.

Section 3 Review

1. What are the four main groups of Latin American people?
2. **Understanding Points of View** Explain why Latin Americans might object to the use of the word "American" to refer only to U.S.citizens.

THE PEOPLE OF LATIN AMERICA

Native Americans were the first people to live in Latin America. Today there are about 30 million Native Americans in the region. They make up the largest group in Bolivia and Peru. Many Native Americans also live in Mexico, Central America, the Andes highlands, and the Amazon valley.

Africans first arrived in Latin America in the 1500s. They came as enslaved people, torn from their homes and forced to work on plantations under brutal conditions. Today, people of African descent live in most areas of Latin America. The largest numbers are in Brazil, Haiti, Cuba, Jamaica, and Venezuela.

Europeans first came to Latin American during the late 1400s. Millions have come since. Early settlers were from Spain and Portugal.

In the late 1800s and early 1900s, many people came to Latin America from Italy and Germany. About a third of all the people in Argentina and Uruguay have Italian backgrounds. Large numbers of people with German backgrounds live in Argentina, Brazil, and Chile.

Mestizos are part Native American and part European. In Mexico and many countries of Central and South America, mestizos make up the largest group. Mulattos have African and European backgrounds. Many of the people in the Dominican Republic, Cuba, Brazil, and other countries are mulattos. Other people are of mixed Native American and African descent.

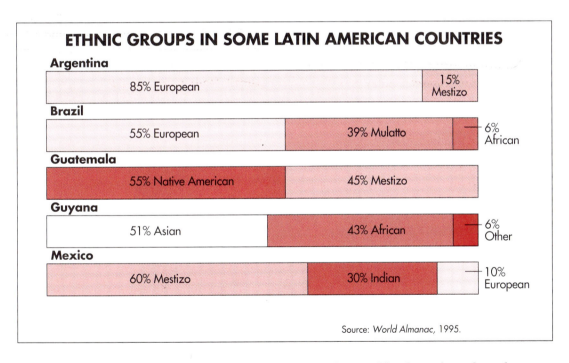

ETHNIC GROUPS IN SOME LATIN AMERICAN COUNTRIES

Argentina
| 85% European | 15% Mestizo |

Brazil
| 55% European | 39% Mulatto | 6% African |

Guatemala
| 55% Native American | 45% Mestizo |

Guyana
| 51% Asian | 43% African | 6% Other |

Mexico
| 60% Mestizo | 30% Indian | 10% European |

Source: *World Almanac*, 1995.

The ethnic backgrounds of Latin Americans are diverse. The chart above shows how the population makeup varies from one Latin American country to another. Because of this diversity, the people in some of Latin America have not been greatly concerned with a person's skin color. In general, education, wealth, and jobs are more important than skin color. However, prejudice based on skin color does exist. Prejudice based on ethnic background is also found. For example, in countries with large Native American populations, the Native Americans are the poorest and least educated.

Living in Different Environments

How do the people of Latin America interact with their environments?

Only a small portion of the land of Latin America can be used for farming and building. Much of the land is covered by mountains and deserts. The Andes Mountains are too high and too cold for large-scale farming. The soils of the rain forest and dry grasslands are poor. The deserts cannot support much life.

Yet for thousands of years, the people of Latin America have made their living from the land. They have done this by adapting their ways of life to the challenges presented by the land.

Rain Forests

A large part of Latin America is tropical rain forest. The largest rain forest is located around the Amazon River. The rain forests have many products that are useful to people in other parts of the world. Wood is one of the most important of these products. Another important product of the rain forest is chicle. It is used to make chewing gum.

In the forest, small groups of Native Americans live in villages near rivers. Growing food is a problem for these people because the soil is poor. Yet the people manage to grow much of their food in small forest clearings. The men clear the land by chopping down trees or burning away the thick brush. Once the land has been cleared, the women plant. The men go into the forest to get more food by hunting and fishing.

The people who live in the rain forest make almost everything they use from the products of the forest. They make their houses from thatch, straw, grass, and leaves. The women weave clothing, mats, and baskets out of grasses and leaves.

World interest in rain forest products and the desire for more land to farm are having a dramatic effect on the rain forests. They are being destroyed at a record rate. The destruction threatens the wildlife and plant life that need the forest to survive. You will read more about this in Chapter 5.

Millions of square miles of Amazon rain forest is covered by tropical trees. Heavy rain and constant heat encourages rapid plant growth.

Farming in a Vertical Climate

As you have learned, the vertical climate zone is widespread throughout Latin America. In this zone, the climate changes with the altitude.

Vertical climate affects the crops a farmer grows. In the hot and damp lowlands of Central America, there are plantations of bananas and cacao (kuh•KOW) beans. Cacao is the bean from which chocolate is made. These crops need the wet, rainy weather and long growing season of the tropics.

In the cool climate of the highlands, the most common crop is coffee. Coffee is grown in the highlands of Brazil and Colombia. Most of the coffee is grown on large estates. Brazil is the world's leading coffee grower. Colombia is the second largest.

Life on the Savanna

The grassland, or savanna, north and south of the Amazon rain forest stretches over parts of Brazil, Venezuela, and Colombia. This area has only two seasons: rainy and dry.

In the grassland, cattle are raised on huge ranches, called haciendas (ah•see•EHN•dahs). The cattle are always on the move. In the dry season, the rivers become little more than streams. Cattle graze near the streams where the grass is still moist and green. In the rainy season, the rivers flood their banks. Then the cowboys drive the cattle to higher land, or mesas, between the swollen rivers.

Life in an Oil Economy

The developed world depends on oil. Some of the richest oil reserves in the world are found in Mexico, Venezuela, and the plains of Ecuador and Peru. Mexico is one of the world's leading producers of oil. Most of its oil is shipped to the United States.

Oil is also a major product of Venezuela. The sale of oil has brought the country much wealth. As a result, the average income of Venezuelans is one of the highest of any people in Latin America. As you will read in Chapter 4, however, that wealth is not spread evenly. There is still much poverty and misery in the cities and villages of Venezuela.

Section 4 Review

1. What products come from the rain forests of Latin America?

2. **Determining Cause and Effect** What is one effect of oil production in Latin America?

The Aymará people live in a barren land in the *altiplano*, or the high plains, of Peru and Bolivia. Few food crops grow on the altiplano. One crop that does grow in this environment is potatoes. The Aymarás eat potatoes at every meal.

The Aymarás: People of the Andes

High in the Andes of South America, the mountains divide into two ranges. Between the ranges, great plains stretch for more than 2,000 miles (3,220 km). The highest part of this plain lies in Peru and Bolivia. In certain places, the plain rises to more than 13,000 feet (3,960 m). One such place is along the border of Peru and Bolivia.

The High Plains

The land along the border is bleak and barren. The winds blow constantly. In winter, the cold wind roars fiercely over the land. In summer, the wind blows up a fine stream of dust. The dust gets on everything — including the lungs of the people who live here. The soil is poor and the grass is thin. Rainfall is light.

In this harsh land live the Aymará (ay•mah•RAH) people. About 100 Aymará villages dot the *altiplano*, or high plain. One of the villages is Chapito, which lies at the end of an ancient Native American trail. Chapito is cut off from other villages by steep hills and deep gorges. It lies in Peru, but in this remote area few people care whether they are in Peru or Bolivia. The people have so little to do with the politics, economy, or culture of either of these countries.

Chapito is a poor village. Almost all the villagers scrape out a living from the dusty land. Some raise *llamas* (YAH•mahz) to carry supplies. These camel-like animals also provide people with wool to make blankets and coats. The llamas survive by eating a brown straw-like grass. Not much else grows in this land.

For hundreds of years, Aymará men have been leaving the villages to work in the mines. At first, they were forced to work in the silver mines of the Spanish. About 100 years ago, as the supply of silver ran low, the Aymarás went to work in the tin mines. Here, they worked under very harsh conditions. Few miners lived to celebrate their thirtieth birthdays. Thousands died in mining accidents.

Farmers and Herders

Today, most Aymarás survive by farming and herding. They grow crops on the poor soil of the plains. Fish from nearby Lake Titicaca adds to their diet.

Potatoes are one of the few foods that grow well at this altitude. The Aymarás eat potatoes at almost every meal. They dry and preserve them for winter. They prepare them every way they know how — roasted, fried, stewed, and steamed.

The Aymarás have their own way of "freeze drying" potatoes. They spread the potatoes out on the ground to freeze at night.

When the sun comes up, the potatoes thaw. The next night, they freeze again. Finally, the Aymarás tramp on the potatoes with their bare feet to squeeze out the last drops of moisture. This leaves a mush called *chuño* (CHOON•yoh), which is used in stews and soups.

On Assignment. . .

The Aymarás might make a good subject for your poster. Focus on their unique way of life as a point of interest on a trip to the Andes.

Family Life

If you had visited an Aymará village 500 years ago, you would have found houses not very different from those in Aymará villages today. These houses are built of a mud-dried brick called adobe. Each house has one room — and no windows! The only opening is a small door. This keeps as much heat as possible inside the house.

Family life is important to the Aymarás. Children learn to perform tasks early in life. At age five, children are sent out to herd a few llamas or lambs. (sheep)

At age 12, boys are sent to work in the fields. By 16 or 17, many boys leave the village to work in the mines.

Life is hard on the altiplano. The cold and the lack of oxygen take their toll on the body. The average baby born on the altiplano can expect to live only about 32 years.

To find an easier life, whole families have moved from the villages to the cities of Lima and La Paz. Lima is the largest city in Peru. La Paz is the largest city in Bolivia. About half the people of La Paz are Native American. Many are Aymarás.

A Proud History — An Independent Future

Though their life is harsh, the Aymarás have a strong sense of pride. They take satisfaction in their history. Aymará stories tell of people who were independent until they were conquered by the Spanish in 1542. Spanish rule was harsh. The Aymarás were forced to work in mines and to send bribes to the Spanish.

In 1780, the Aymarás rebelled. Forty years of bloody war followed. Finally, in 1821, the Spanish gave up the war. The Aymarás became independent again. When the countries of Bolivia and Peru were formed, their border cut across Aymará land. But lines on a map mean little to the Aymarás. Out on the altiplano, they scratch a living out of a barren land regardless of what country they live in.

Case Study Review

1. What is the altiplano?
2. **Comparing and Contrasting** How are the lives of young Aymarás different from your life?

I. Reviewing Vocabulary

Match each word on the left with the correct definition on the right.

1. volcano
2. peninsula
3. tropics
4. mestizos

   a. land that is surrounded on three sides by water
   b. a mountain from which hot melted rocks, ash, and gases sometimes flow
   c. people who are part Native American and part European
   d. lands that are near the equator

II. Understanding the Chapter

Answer the questions below on a separate sheet of paper.

1. What are the major geographic features of each of Latin America's four regions?
2. What is a vertical climate? Describe how a vertical climate affects how people live on the land.
3. In what two general areas do most of the people of Latin America live? Why?
4. Why are many Aymarás leaving their traditional villages for the city?

III. Building Skills: Studying Maps

Study the maps on pages 101 and 102. Then answer the following questions.

1. Which countries of South America are north of the equator? Which are south?
2. What is the largest country in Latin America in terms of size?
3. What are the chief bodies of water that border Latin America?
4. Name three Latin American nations that are on islands.

IV. Working Together

With a small group, write a television script about a Latin American culture. For example, you may choose to write about the life of the Aymarás on the altiplano of Peru. Before you begin writing, brainstorm and outline ideas for the show. Be sure to include information about Aymará traditions and history.

On Assignment. . .

Creating Posters: Review the notes you took as you read the chapter. Sketch out your ideas for travel posters on sheets of paper. Create messages to appear on your posters. Choose the best sketch and message and transfer your idea to a large piece of paper. Present your work to your teacher or to the class. Include a paragraph or two explaining how your poster will attract tourists to Latin America.

The Early Civilizations of Latin America

Which civilizations existed in Latin America before the European conquest?

People from early Mexican cultures are shown crafting gold and feather works in this colorful mural by the modern Mexican painter, Diego Rivera.

Looking at Key Terms

- **glacier** a huge sheet of ice
- **nomads** people who have no permanent home and move from place to place in search of food and water
- **irrigation** a system of human-made ditches that carry water
- **pyramid** a building that is rectangular at its base with four triangular sides that meet at the top in a point
- **drought** a long period without rain
- **causeway** a raised road across water or marshland
- **aqueduct** a system of pipes that carry water to where it is needed
- **immune** protected against a specific disease

On Assignment. . .

Keeping a Journal: The chapter you are about to read describes three major empires that existed in Latin America hundreds of years ago. Imagine that you have the opportunity to travel through these empires. On your journey, you will keep a journal to record your impressions of these three civilizations. As you read the chapter, take notes for your journal entries. Look for several hints placed throughout the chapter that will help you gather your notes. At the end of the chapter, you will organize your notes and put together your journal entries.

The First Americans

Who were the first Americans and where did they come from?

Have you ever thought about what your town or city was like hundreds or even thousands of years ago? Perhaps you've wondered what kind of people lived there and what those people did for a living.

Scientists have thought about those very same things. In this chapter, you will learn some of what they have found. You will also learn about the major civilizations of early Latin America.

Settling a Continent

About 30,000 years ago, nearly one third of the world was covered with huge sheets of ice. These ice sheets are called **glaciers** (GLAY•shuhrz). It was a time known as the ice age. During this time, a narrow strip of land connected Asia and North America across what is now called the Bering Sea.

Herds of Asian moose and other animals began to cross this strip of land. Hunters followed the animals. Scientists believe that these hunters were the first people to live in the Americas.

This movement of people from Asia to America did not take place all at once. It occurred over thousands of years. It ended when the glaciers finally melted. Then the sea once more covered the land between the two continents.

The first Americans lived as **nomads.** They moved from place to place in search of animals to hunt. Many traveled through parts of what is now called North America. Others drifted southward, settling in Mexico and Central America. In the years to come, some people continued on into South America.

Farming Develops

Over thousands of years, the hunters learned new ways of life. People living around lakes and rivers began to fish. Others ground seeds to make flour, or gathered berries, nuts, and bulbs.

Then people in the area of Mexico made a key discovery. They learned that when the seeds of wild plants are placed in the ground, new plants will grow. This was the discovery of farming. Farming changed the way many Native Americans lived. With food from crops, many groups stopped being nomads. Over many years, Native American farming villages were established all over North and South America.

Another major development was **irrigation.** This is a system of human-made ditches that carried water from streams to the fields. Irrigation was important because it allowed farmers to water their crops during the dry season.

Civilizations Emerge

The discovery of farming led to other developments. Farming made food supplies more predictable. Fewer people died of hunger. Populations increased. Also, as the size of farms grew, not everyone in the village had to farm in order to eat. Therefore, some people farmed while others focused on other work such as pottery or toolmaking.

After a time, small villages grew into larger communities. Governments were formed to organize these communities. Religion became more complex as people looked for explanations of the mysteries of life. Priests and other religious officials took charge of rituals and ceremonies that marked the seasons of the year and the passage of people through time.

Over the years, powerful city-states and empires appeared. Three of the greatest empires in Latin America were the Mayan, the Aztec, and the Incan.

1. Why did people first come to the Americas?

2. **Understanding Cause and Effect** How did the development of farming lead to the creation of large communities?

SECTION 2

The Mysterious Mayas

Who were the Mayas and where did they live?

Deep in the rain forests of Guatemala, the city of Tikal (tee•KAHL) lay hidden. For a thousand years, the city sat empty. Trees and vines grew around and over the buildings.

The Glory of Tikal

There was a time when Tikal was a thriving city. Around A.D. 600, more than 40,000 people lived there. At the center of Tikal, huge **pyramids** soared to the skies. A pyramid is a building that has a rectangular base and triangular sides that usually rise to a point. Mayan pyramids, however, were flat on top.

Near the pyramids was a huge market. At the market, people traded goods such as food, pottery, leather hides, and jewelry.

Around Tikal's pyramids were the palaces of rulers and wealthy people. These palaces had many rooms built around courtyards. At the outskirts of town were canals to bring the water to farmland during the dry season.

For about 200 years, Tikal was the largest city of the people known as the Mayas. But by A.D. 800, Tikal had begun to decline. About 100 years later, Tikal lay abandoned.

What caused Tikal's decline? Experts don't know for sure. But they have many theories

Huge pyramids lay buried in the rain forests of Mexico and Guatemala for a thousand years. They testify to the glories of Mayan civilization.

about what happened to the mysterious city of the Mayas. Some of these theories will unfold in this section.

Mayan Cities

Mayan civilization developed in the rain forests of Guatemala. By about 300 B.C., the Mayas were building cities. The Mayas built about 40 cities with more than 20,000 people in each. Tikal was the greatest Mayan city.

The Mayan cities served as religious centers. These religious centers had many steep flat-topped pyramids. Graceful stone temples stood atop these pyramids.

Religion was a very important part of Mayan life. The Mayas believed that the earth had been created and destroyed four or five times. They believed that it would be destroyed again. To persuade the gods to delay destruction, Mayan rulers prayed and sacrificed prisoners. *Sacrifice* means "to kill as a way of pleasing the gods."

Seers of the Stars

The Mayas were experts at mathematics. They also carefully studied the heavens and the movements of the stars and planets. They used their knowledge to develop an accurate calendar of 365 days. The calendar helped the Mayas predict solar eclipses. A solar eclipse occurs when the light of the sun is blocked by the moon.

The Decline of the Mayas

Mayan civilization was at its height between A.D. 300 and 900. Around the year 800, the Mayas suddenly abandoned their great cities in Guatemala and moved northward into the Yucatán peninsula. The reasons for this move are unknown. Experts have suggested a number of possibilities. Among them are a sudden change in climate, a civil war, or a foreign invasion.

During the years in Yucatán, the Mayas began to rebuild. Their new empire reached great heights. Beginning around 1100, however, the Mayas were weakened by **drought**, a long period without rain. The Mayas also faced attacks from other Native Americans.

Mayan civilization continued to decline for a few hundred years. Finally, it came to an end when the Mayas were conquered by the Spanish in 1546.

Today, the great cities of the Mayas are only beautiful ruins. However, several million people who are descendants of the Mayas live in Guatemala and Mexico.

Section 2 Review

1. What theories have scientists used to explain the decline of Mayan civilization?

2. **Formulating Questions** Imagine that you could speak to an ancient Maya. What one question would you most like to ask that person? Explain why you would ask this question.

SECTION 3

The Golden Empire of the Aztecs

How did the Aztecs build a great empire in the valley of Mexico?

For weeks, the emperor Montezuma (mahn•tuh•ZOO•mah) had shut himself off from the world. He remained in his palace. He spoke to no one but his closest advisers. Day after day, he sat silently by a window looking out over his great city.

Montezuma was the ruler of the powerful Aztec empire. He was the most powerful person on earth — or so he thought. Yet he was frightened by a small band of light-skinned strangers. Were they enemies? Did they mean to destroy him? Or were they the light-skinned gods of Aztec legend that had come to reward the Aztec people?

Finally, Montezuma reached a decision. He summoned the great lords of the land. They were suspicious of the strangers and were eager to destroy them. They needed only a word from Montezuma.

But the word, when it came, was disappointing. The leader of these strangers may be the light-skinned god of legend, Montezuma said. The Aztecs would treat the strangers with respect and invite them to come to the Aztec capital. So began the downfall of the mighty Aztec empire.

The Eagle and the Snake

More than 300 years before Montezuma's rule, the Aztecs were a wandering band of poor warriors. They were so poor that they traveled from place to place, fighting for anyone who would pay them. Around A.D. 1200, they entered the Central Valley of Mexico. The valley runs down the center of the modern-day nation of Mexico.

According to legend, an Aztec god told them to wander until they came to a place where an eagle was eating a snake. After many years of wandering, the Aztecs saw

Montezuma, emperor of the Aztecs, one night saw a blazing comet. It was an omen of death both for the emperor and for his powerful empire.

On Assignment. . .

For your journal, imagine that you traveled through the city of Tenochtitlán at its height. What do you find most impressive about the city? What similarities and differences does it have to the place where you live?

their sign on an island in a shallow lake. In about 1325, they began to build a settlement there.

As their power grew, the Aztecs needed more land. They increased the size of their islands by pouring land into the lake until the islands almost touched. They built **causeways,** or raised roadways, to connect the islands. The Aztecs called their city Tenochtitlán (teh•nahch•tee•TLAHN).

As time passed, Tenochtitlán grew into a large and beautiful city. It had great pyramids, broad avenues, and handsome buildings. The Aztecs built a system of **aqueducts,** pipes that carry water to where it is needed. Tenochtitlán had large parks and even a zoo. At the height of its power, over 300,000 people lived in Tenochtitlán.

The Aztecs Build an Empire

As the years passed, the Aztecs extended their rule over their neighbors. The conquered peoples were forced to work for the Aztecs. They also had to pay heavy taxes. Defeated cities were forced to send gold, jewels, animal skins, and food to the Aztecs. Worse, they had to send men and women.

Many of these men and women were sacrificed to Aztec gods. Prisoners taken in battle were also sacrificed.

As more territory was conquered, the Aztec empire became wealthy. By 1519, Montezuma ruled a land of 35 provinces. In it lived about 25 million people. Montezuma commanded an army of as many as 200,000 soldiers.

Then, one day in March 1519, messengers raced to the city with startling news. A small group of light-skinned strangers had landed on the east coast. The pale-skinned men rode strange animals that looked like deer but made noises like dragons. These animals were horses, which the Aztecs had never seen before. The messengers also reported that the men had weapons that fired iron balls.

The light-skinned strangers were Europeans. The Aztecs did not know it then, but the end of their empire was close at hand.

Section 3 Review

1. Why did the news of strangers in the east frighten Montezuma?

2. **Making Inferences** Do you think that the people the Aztecs conquered felt any loyalty toward Montezuma or the Aztec empire? Why or why not?

The Incas: People of the Sun

How did the Incas use science to build an empire?

While the Aztecs were building their empire in Mexico, another group was creating a great civilization in South America. This group was the Incas.

The Incas were scientific farmers. They farmed the dry areas along the Pacific coast by building irrigation systems. These brought water to the fields from more than 100 miles (166 km) away. They learned to use fertilizers and crop rotation. They cut terraces on the mountain slopes to increase the amount of land they could farm. The terraces kept the soil from washing away. Incan rulers ordered farmers to put part of their crops in public storehouses. In drought years, when the farming was bad, crops from the storehouses were given to the needy.

The religion of the Incas was based on sun worship. The Incas believed that their emperor, called the Lord Inca, was descended from the sun. Eventually, all people of the empire were called Incas, or "children of the sun."

The Incas lived in the Andes highlands. In about A.D. 1200, they spread their rule over other groups in the area. By the late 1400s, they had conquered many of the peoples of South America. Their empire covered much of present-day Peru, Ecuador, Bolivia, and Chile. At its height, the Incan empire had a population of about 12 million people.

The Master Builders

The capital of the empire was Cuzco (KOOS•koh). Incan rulers worked hard to unify the people of their vast empire. Conquered people had to learn the Incan language, Quechua (KECH•wah). Incan nobles were sent to live among newly conquered people to teach them Incan customs and

Machu Picchu, an ancient city of the Incas, was built high up in the Andes Mountains. The city lay hidden for many years until it was rediscovered in the 1800s.

laws. They established schools that taught the Incan religion. Unlike groups conquered by the Aztecs, groups conquered by the Incas tended to be loyal.

The Incas were great builders. They built a vast system of roads connecting all parts of the empire. Ten thousand miles of roads and bridges stretched from the Pacific Ocean across the Andes to the Amazon River. Some of these roads are still in use today. Besides roads and bridges, the Incas built great temples and palaces. Their builders were so skilled that they fitted stone blocks together without cement.

Decline of the Incan Empire

In the early 1500s, the Incan empire was divided by civil war. In 1525, the Incan ruler died, and his two sons fought for control of the empire. Although one son eventually won, the fighting took its toll. When the light-skinned strangers arrived in 1533, they found the Incan empire greatly weakened.

Section 4 Review

1. What advances did the Incas bring to farming?
2. **Comparing and Contrasting** How did Incan rulers differ from the Aztecs in the way they treated the people they conquered?

SECTION 5

The European Conquest

Why did the Europeans come to the Americas?

While the Aztec and Incan civilizations were reaching new heights, the people of Europe were beginning to sail the seas on a grand scale. In the 1400s, Spain and Portugal competed fiercely with one another to find all-sea trade routes to Asia. Asia was the source of rich trade goods such as silks and spices.

In the late 1400s, Portugal established a water route to Asia around the coast of Africa. Spain had put its faith in an Italian sea captain named Christopher Columbus. Columbus had convinced the Spanish queen, Isabella, to support a wild idea. He wanted to reach Asia by sailing west across the Atlantic. Most people thought the idea was foolish, but the queen backed him anyway.

Instead of Asia, of course, Columbus reached the Americas. No one in Europe knew these huge lands existed. Between 1492 and 1504, Columbus made four voyages to the Americas. During his second voyage, he began the first European settlement there. Other explorers working for Spain extended the conquests.

Conquest of the Mainland

By 1500, there were a number of Spanish settlements on the islands of the West Indies. Once the Spanish began settling down, they brought all sorts of European goods to the Americas. These goods included horses, cattle, sheep, citrus fruits, and sugar cane — none of which existed in the Americas. The Spanish also brought goods from the Americas back to Europe. These included potatoes, corn, tobacco, tomatoes, green peppers, and chocolate.

From their island forts, soldiers were sent to explore the nearby coasts in search of riches.

The Fall of the Aztecs and the Incas
In 1519, Hernán Cortés (kor•TEHZ) landed with a small force on the coast of Mexico. It was Cortés's landing that so worried Montezuma, the leader of the Aztecs. On the coast, Cortés learned of the Aztec belief that a light-skinned god would come to save them.

Making certain to approach from the east, as the god was supposed to do, Cortés and his forces arrived in the Aztec capital in November. They captured and imprisoned Montezuma. For a while, Cortés tried to rule through the emperor. He thought that this would be the easiest way to control the Aztecs. However, by 1520, many Aztecs began to reject the idea that the Spanish were gods. They saw them simply as greedy men who could not seem to get enough gold. The Aztecs launched an attack on the Spanish, killing half of them. In the struggle,

The Spanish, left, were heavily outnumbered by the Aztecs, right. But the Spanish had modern weapons, which devastated the Aztecs who used old-fashioned weapons.

Montezuma died. Cortés escaped at night with the rest of his forces.

In 1521, Cortés returned, leading a force of about 1,000 Spanish soldiers and many Native American allies. These Native Americans had been conquered by the Aztecs and were eager to fight against them. They believed that once the Spanish defeated the Aztecs, they would be free.

After a three-month siege, the Aztecs surrendered. The city of Tenochtitlán was destroyed, and Cortés began to ship Aztec treasures back to Spain.

In 1532, Francisco Pizarro sailed southward along the west coast of South America and arrived at the Incan empire. Pizarro captured the Incan chief and killed him. The Incas were soon defeated. The Spanish were now masters of two treasure houses in Latin America — Mexico and Peru. Other conquerors pushed Spanish control throughout Latin America.

Spain's Rivalry With Portugal

Before long, both Spain and Portugal claimed lands in the Americas. These countries asked the Pope — the head of the Roman Catholic Church — to divide the Americas between them. In 1493, the Pope drew an imaginary line running north and south on the map. All lands west of this line would belong to Spain. All lands east of this line would belong to Portugal. Because of this agreement, Portugal later claimed the land that is now Brazil.

Section 5 Review

1. How did Christopher Columbus propose to get to Asia?

2. **Understanding Points of View** Why do you suppose that Spain was more interested than Portugal in sailing west to reach Asia?

Why the Aztec Empire Fell:
The Real Story

As you read on pages 29–30, the Aztecs crushed a Spanish force led by Hernán Cortés in July 1520. After that the Aztecs thought they were safe.

Yet little over a year later, the Aztec empire was in ruins. The Spanish were in total control. How did this happen?

Aztec Enemies

Cortés knew that many of the people that the Aztecs had conquered hated them. Cortés played on this anger. He promised to help free the conquered people from Aztec rule. He soon won many allies.

When Cortés first marched into Tenochtitlán in 1519, thousands of Native American soldiers marched with him. They thought that once the Aztecs were defeated, the Spanish would leave.

The Power of Disease

Unknowingly, Spain had an even more destructive weapon than its forces. That weapon was disease. The Spanish carried to the Americas diseases that were common in Europe. Among them were measles, mumps, and smallpox. These diseases were unknown in the Americas. No one there was **immune** to them. The word *immune* means "protected against disease."

Spanish soldiers who marched with Cortés in 1520 carried one of these European diseases, <u>smallpox</u>. Soon smallpox raged through the Native American population in Mexico. The disease killed nobles and slaves, soldiers and farmers, adults and children. The Aztec government and army were badly weakened.

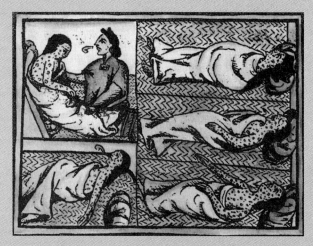

Smallpox destroyed the Aztec people. One Aztec said, "The illness was so dreadful that no one could walk or move. So they simply starved to death in their beds."

The Last Battle

After the death of Montezuma, an Aztec noble ruled briefly. He, however, died of smallpox. Then a 22-year-old noble named Cuauhtémoc (kwow•TEH•mohk) became emperor. Cuauhtémoc was a cousin of Montezuma. He would be the last Aztec ruler.

Cuauhtémoc tried to rally his people to defeat the Spanish. He asked a nearby city for help. The neighboring people were not moved by his plea. The leader of the city told Cuauhtémoc, "How would I gain by sending men to you, for we are always at war. Let the strangers kill the Aztec."

In May 1521, the Spanish attacked again. There were 900 Spanish soldiers and 100,000 Native American allies. Soon, Tenochtitlán was sealed off. No food or supplies could enter.

Still, the Aztecs fought on. The Spanish had to take the city house by house. For 93 days the Aztecs resisted.

Finally, on August 13, 1521, the battle was over. There was no longer a city to fight for. Tenochtitlán lay in ruins.

The Last Aztec Emperor

Cuauhtémoc survived the battle. He was taken prisoner and brought to Cortés. The Aztec prisoner spoke to his conqueror.

I have done everything in my power to defend myself and my people, and everything that it was my duty to do. You may do with me whatever you wish. So kill me, for that will be best.

Cortés did not kill Cuauhtémoc then. The Spanish kept Cuauhtémoc as a prisoner. They tortured him, hoping that he would reveal where to find more Aztec gold.

Cortés feared that if Cuauhtémoc escaped, he might lead an uprising of the Aztecs. In 1525, Cortés led a campaign into Central America. On the way, Cortés charged that Cuauhtémoc had tried to start a rebellion. Far from his home, Cuauhtémoc was hanged by the Spanish.

Cuauhtémoc's courage made him a hero to Mexico's people. Today, a statue of him stands in Mexico City, not far from where his palace once stood. It is a monument to the last emperor of the Aztec nation.

Case Study Review

1. Who was Cuauhtémoc?
2. **Understanding Points of View** Why do you suppose that Spanish histories of the conquest emphasize the heroic role of Spanish soldiers, rather than the spread of disease?

I. Reviewing Vocabulary

Match each word on the left with the correct definition on the right.

1. causeway   **a.** a long period without rain
2. aqueduct   **b.** a system of pipes that carry water to where it is needed
3. drought   **c.** system of human-made ditches that carry water
4. irrigation   **d.** a raised road across water or marshland

II. Understanding the Chapter

Answer the questions below on a separate sheet of paper.

1. In Section 2 of this chapter, Mayan culture is described as being very advanced. Give two examples of this advanced culture.
2. Why did the Aztecs decide to settle and build the city of Tenochtitlán?
3. Describe Incan accomplishments in building and farming.
4. What foods did the Spanish bring to the Americas and take back to Europe?

III. Building Skills: Making a Chart

Copy the chart below into your notebook. Fill in the approximate dates and major accomplishments of each of the three civilizations discussed in this chapter.

Civilization	Approximate Dates	Major Accomplishments
Maya		
Aztec		
Inca		

IV. Working Together

Form a small group with three or four of your classmates. With the group, think of an important event or accomplishment described in this chapter. Create a cartoon book about the event or accomplishment. Be sure to give full details about whatever you show.

On Assignment...

Keeping a Journal: Review the notes that you took as you read this chapter. Then create several journal entries that describe your thoughts and feelings about the early civilizations of Latin America. Read your journal entries to a classmate. Then discuss any similarities and differences in your impressions of these early civilizations.

CHAPTER 3

Breaking the Grip of the Crown

Why did Latin American nations seek independence?

Built on the foundations of an Aztec temple, Mexico City's Cathedral symbolized a new city. "Mexico City," Cortés said, "will soon be the most noble in the known world."

On Assignment. . .

Creating a Mini-History:
Work with two or three classmates to create an illustrated mini-history for third grade students. Your mini-histories will contain three chapters about life in Latin America and the struggle for independence. As you read this chapter, note topics that you think would make interesting chapters for third graders. Consider featuring action-packed events, interesting characters, and good stories. Also, look for hint boxes providing suggestions to complete your assignment. At the end of the chapter, you will be given further instructions on how to complete your project.

Looking at Key Terms

- **Middle Passage** the journey across the Atlantic Ocean from West Africa to the Americas that was the route of the African American slave trade
- **mission** a religious settlement devoted to spreading Christianity
- **Creole** a person in Spanish Latin America whose parents or ancestors were from Spain
- **peon** a poor person who works all his or her life for rich landowners
- **viceroy** a person who governs a colony as a representative of the king or queen

Building a Great Empire

How was Spain's empire in the Americas organized?

One summer day in 1566, the people of Mexico City watched as wagon after wagon passed them in the street. Each wagon was loaded with a fortune in silver. Armed guards rode beside the wagons. The wagons were headed east — to the port of Veracruz.

In Veracruz, merchants waited for the first sight of the Spanish fleet. News that the ships were near meant that it was time for the great silver fair to begin. For 20 days, merchants of New Spain would trade their silver for furniture, glassware, and the latest fashions from Spain.

When the fair was over, the silver would be loaded onto the Spanish boats. Within weeks, much of the silver would be safely locked in the vaults of the king of Spain. The flow of silver and gold from its Latin American colonies made Spain the richest country in Europe. It also made Mexico City a wealthy city.

Slavery in the Spanish Empire

Spain's empire in the Americas grew over a number of years. Much of its growth was due to the labor of the people it ruled.

Native Americans made up much of the work force. They were forced to work on Spanish plantations and in mines. Disease and too much hard labor killed thousands of Native Americans.

The Spanish began to look for other ways to fill their need for free or cheap labor. Soon enslaved Africans were being shipped to the Americas under brutal conditions for this purpose. Millions made the forced journey.

The slave trade left memories of misery from Africa to the Caribbean. Countless Africans died in the horrible journey across the Atlantic known as the **Middle Passage.**

Sugar cane was harvested by enslaved Africans. Why was the labor of enslaved people from West Africa so important to the Spanish colonies?

On the trip, chained Africans were packed together in cargo holds swarming with rats. One enslaved African later reported that the white men tore babies from their mothers' arms and threw them overboard. Two mothers leaped into the water after their children. One drowned. The other threw herself overboard one night.

By the mid-1500s, there were more enslaved Africans than Europeans on some Caribbean islands. To control the enslaved Africans, the Spanish used cruel means of punishment. Yet Africans endured the heartless treatment and managed to keep some of their traditions alive. Over time, African and

On Assignment...

One chapter of your mini-history could describe the Middle Passage. What images and words came to mind as you read about the journey of enslaved Africans? Use those thoughts in your mini-history.

Spanish ways mixed with those of Native Americans. This produced the unique cultures of the Caribbean region.

Organizing the Colonies

As the colonies prospered, Spanish settlers established new towns. By royal order, these new towns were all built in the same pattern.

The heart of every Spanish town was the main square, or plaza. In the plaza, people met for business or pleasure. The plaza still serves the same purposes in many Latin American and Spanish towns today.

The most important building in the Spanish town was the church. Sometimes the church faced the plaza. Other times, it was built on higher ground and could be seen for miles around. On the other sides of the plaza were the town hall and other public buildings.

The Role of the Church

One of the goals of the Roman Catholic Church was to get Native Americans and African Americans to become Christians. The church established **missions,** religious settlements devoted to spreading Christianity. The church tried to teach the Spanish language and customs. Some church leaders also tried to protect Native Americans from cruel treatment.

The Catholics of the Jesuit order set up missions along the Paraná River. For more than 150 years, Jesuits worked with the Guaraní (gwah•rah•NEE), Native Americans in Paraguay, Argentina, Uruguay, and Brazil.

In time, the Jesuits founded more than 30 missions devoted to converting Guaraní. They taught Guaraní to read and write. They also helped set up a Guaraní army to fight slave-hunting bands. Before this army formed, thousands of Guaraní were captured and taken to slave markets in Brazil.

On the other hand, the missions put Native Americans to work for the benefit of the religious orders. Native Americans provided the labor to build churches and raise food. The missions added a great deal of wealth to the Roman Catholic Church. This helped make the church the largest landowner in the Americas.

Social Order in Spanish America

The Spanish American colonies had a rigid social order. In Spanish America, a person was born into a class and remained there for life. There was almost no chance to move from one class to another.

At the top were people who had been born in Spain. They controlled most of the power and wealth. They held the highest offices in the church and the government. These people looked down on other people in the colonies.

Slightly lower on the scale were the **Creoles.** They were people born of Spanish parents in the Americas. The Creoles could not hold important positions in the government. But many were very

The conquered people of Mexico were put to work creating cities for the Spanish. Here, the city of Vera Cruz is being built.

wealthy. Some owned silver mines or huge country estates.

Many Creoles resented the power of the Spanish. Tensions between the classes would lead to revolutions during the 1800s.

Mestizos were people of mixed Spanish and Native American ancestry. They had no voice in the colonial government. However, they did many of the skilled jobs in Spanish colonies. They tended small farms and stores. Many also sold handmade goods.

Mulattos made up another group. These were people who had one parent of European descent and one of African descent. Some mulattos were accepted by mestizos or Africans as social equals. They were not accepted by the Spanish or by Creoles.

At the bottom of society were Native Americans and enslaved Africans. These groups lived in extreme poverty. Many toiled from sunrise to sundown. They lived in small huts with few pieces of furniture.

Destroying Native American Life

The Native Americans who survived conquest and disease were an important part of the labor force. Native peoples built mansions and churches for Spanish officials. They tilled the soil and mined for silver. They performed most of the basic tasks of colonial life.

Many Native Americans received wages for their work. But the wages were so low that workers had to borrow heavily from landowners to buy seed, farming equipment, and other necessities. In order to repay the debt, they were forced to become **peons.** Most Native Americans worked all their lives for landowners and were never able to pay off the debt.

The Spanish attempted to wipe out Native American culture. In missions, priests taught Native Americans to speak Spanish and to follow the Roman Catholic faith. Native Americans who worked on farms for Spanish landowners were forced to wear European-style clothing.

As they tried to change Native American culture, the Spanish found that their own culture in the Americas had also changed. The Spanish added such Native American foods as potatoes and corn to their diets. They also added Native American words to their language. Slowly, Spanish and Native American cultures blended. This blending produced the mestizo culture that is widespread in modern-day Mexico.

The Portuguese in Brazil

As you read in Chapter 2, Portugal controlled the region now known as Brazil. Brazil was a rich source of brazilwood — a wood from which red dyes could be made — and sugar cane.

Because of its favorable soil and climate, northeastern Brazil soon became the site of enormous sugar plantations. Enslaved Africans worked the sugar fields under harsh conditions.

In the 1700s, gold and diamonds were discovered inland. This led to a rush of settlement. Thousands of people left the coast hoping to get rich. Thousands more came from Portugal. New towns sprang up almost overnight.

Section 1 Review

1. Describe the way in which towns in Spanish America were built.

2. **Evaluating Information** Consider the following: Today in Paraguay, most people claim some Guaraní ancestry, and the Guaraní language is spoken by 90 percent of the population. Ninety-five percent of Paraguay's population is Roman Catholic. What role do you think the Jesuits played in preserving Guaraní heritage? What aspects of Guaraní heritage did the Jesuits change?

Sor Juana: A Woman in Latin America

In the 1600s, Mexico City was a center of the Spanish empire. In the city, carriages trimmed in gold clattered down stone streets. Bells rang in cathedrals. Students attended classes at the University of Mexico.

During this period, people in Latin America and in Europe admired the author of these words:

*Costliness and wealth bring me
no pleasure; the only happiness I
care to find
derives from setting treasure in
my mind,
and not from mind that's set on
treasure.*

The author was a lonely nun who cared little for the splendor of Mexico City. She wanted only to study and to write poetry. She was known as Sor, or Sister, Juana.

According to legend, Juana Inés de la Cruz (HWAH•nah ee•NEHS deh•lah•kroos) began to read at age three. As a teenager, she wanted to go to the university, but women were not allowed to attend. She begged her mother to let her dress as a man so that she could attend the university anyway. Horrified, her mother refused. That left Juana with two choices. She could marry, or she could become a nun. — *female in a religious order*

When she was 17, Juana chose to become a nun. She thought that life at the convent would give her time to study and write. Because she was a nun, her poetry came to the attention of church officials. Many of them thought it was wrong for a woman to have such intellectual interests as writing poetry. When she criticized a sermon, one church official demanded that she stop writing.

The anger of church officials finally broke Juana's spirit. She gave up writing poetry and sent officials a letter using her blood as ink. In the letter, she renewed her vows as a nun. In 1695, at age 43, Sor Juana died. *Vow pledge*

Case Study Review

1. Why couldn't Sor Juana attend the university?
2. **Analyzing Poetry** What does the poem above say about Sor Juana's beliefs and interests?

Struggle for Independence

How did the nations of Latin America gain independence?

Spain and Portugal were not the only European countries with colonies in Latin America. France, Britain, and the Netherlands also won territories in the region. (See the map below.) These European powers tried to keep tight control over their colonies. But the people who lived in the colonies grew more and more independent. One by one, the colonies began to fight for freedom.

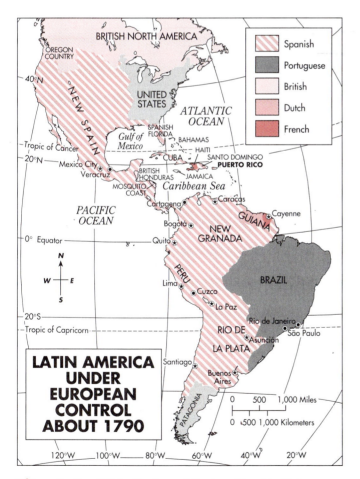

Place By the 1790s, Spain and Portugal had built large empires in the Americas. Who controlled Guiana in 1790? What name was used for Mexico in 1790?

Toussaint L'Ouverture was a self-educated former slave. He took charge of Haiti's independence struggle and defeated the French in a number of battles.

Haiti's Fight for Freedom

The first Latin American war for independence was fought against France. In 1791, enslaved Africans who worked on Haiti's sugar plantations revolted against colonial rule. They were led by a former slave named Toussaint L'Ouverture (loo•ver•TOOR). L'Ouverture had escaped slavery and educated himself. He was one of the main leaders in the fight against French rule. In 1802, he was captured. He died that year in a French prison.

However, the struggle for independence continued. By 1804, the Haitians had driven out the French, and Haiti became the first independent Latin American country.

Resentment in Spain's Colonies

Independence for Spain's colonies came later and not all at once. Colonists fought for freedom for a number of reasons. The system of colonial government was one of those reasons.

Colonial government in Spanish America was very rigid. Spanish America was ruled by **viceroys.** Viceroys were appointed by the Spanish king or queen to rule in his or her place. The viceroy's job was to carry out the orders of the king or queen. A court appointed by the king and queen made sure the viceroy did his job.

The Spanish king and queen and a group of advisers in Spain made all the laws for their American colonies. Because all the decision making took place in Spain, it took a long time to bring about even small changes in the Americas. Also, colonial governments were often corrupt. Wealthy landowners often bribed officials to look the other way when they broke the law.

Another problem was hostility between classes. This was a serious problem by the 1800s. People who had been born in Spain continued to hold the highest positions. Creoles resented this power. Although they were often wealthy landowners, the Creoles were not permitted to hold high positions in government.

First Steps Toward Independence

One event that sparked revolution in Latin America was the American Revolution. The fact that British colonists in North America had won independence from Britain inspired Latin American revolutionaries to get rid of the Spanish.

In Spain's colonies, the movement for independence began on September 16, 1810, in the tiny Mexican village of Dolores. On that day, a local priest called for revolt against Spanish rule. His name was Father Miguel Hidalgo (ee•DAHL•goh).

Hidalgo led an army of thousands of mestizos and Native Americans against Spanish rule. Within a year, the Spanish captured Hidalgo. He was executed in 1811. But other leaders kept up the fight. After ten years of fighting, the rebels ended Spanish rule in Mexico.

Across the Andes

Most Latin American nations had to fight long and hard to break away from European rulers. Like the struggle in Mexico, the fight for independence in Central and South America would take years.

One such fight began in June 1819, when an army of more than 2,000 soldiers struggled to cross the Andes Mountains. They had set out from Venezuela and were marching toward the city of Bogotá in Colombia. There they hoped to surprise the Spanish army.

The leader of the army was Simón Bolívar (boh•LEE•vahr). Bolívar was a wealthy Creole. He had been educated in Europe. There he was inspired by the ideals of the French Revolution and vowed to free South America from Spanish rule.

Bolívar marched his army over the Andes. The soldiers climbed higher and higher into

Simón Bolívar was given the name "The Liberator." Bolívar led Latin Americans to freedom in the northern part of South America.

the snowy mountains. They suffered terribly from the bitter mountain cold.

Despite many hardships, the rebel army made it across. On August 7, 1819, the small army faced 3,000 veteran Spanish troops. A fierce battle followed. In it, the Spanish lost more than 1,000 soldiers. The rebels had won a key battle in Latin America's struggle for independence.

Soon after his victory, Bolívar established the republic of Gran Colombia. It was made up of the present-day countries of Venezuela, Ecuador, Colombia, and Panama.

While Bolívar led the struggle for independence in the northern part of South America, José de San Martín (sahn mahr•TEEN) led it in the southern part. For years, the struggle went back and forth. The rebels made some gains. Then they were defeated by the Spanish. Over time, San Martín continued the struggle and finally won. First, he freed his native land, Argentina. Then he led his army over the Andes into Chile. In 1818, Chile won its independence.

From Chile, San Martín's forces sailed north to Peru. San Martín captured the Spanish stronghold of Lima, but he could not drive the Spanish out of the nearby mountains. San Martín then joined forces with Bolívar. In 1824, they finally drove the Spanish out of Peru. By 1844, all that remained of Spain's once huge empire in the Americas was Cuba and Puerto Rico.

After Independence

Simón Bolívar and other leaders had dreamed of organizing Latin America into one large federal republic like the United States. However, the end of the Spanish empire did not unify Latin America. Vast distances, towering mountains, and thick rain forests separated different parts of South America. Also, the regions had no history of working together. Under Spanish rule, each region had been ruled by its own viceroy. In 1830, Bolívar died bitter that he could not unite South America.

After Bolívar's death, Gran Colombia split into three nations. Central America, which had joined Mexico in 1821, divided into five republics.

The revolutions in Latin America did not change the class system much. The Creoles became the new ruling class. Mestizos and Native Americans had also fought for independence. However, they remained as oppressed as before, being barred from holding high positions in the government, church, and private industry.

The wars of independence caused much damage. Cities filled with poor people who had been thrown off the land by the fighting.

Creole leaders drew up constitutions modeled on the U.S. Constitution. But with no experience in self-government, they had

Region The map of Latin America in 1828 was far different from the map today. In what way was Mexico in 1828 different from Mexico today?

trouble getting their plans to work. Latin America now faced the challenge of building new governments and new economies.

Brazil

In Brazil, independence was won without bloodshed. In 1807, Emperor Napoleon of France invaded Spain and attacked Portugal. The royal family of Portugal fled to Brazil. Once there, the king declared Brazil a kingdom. The king returned to Portugal after Napoleon was defeated. His son Pedro stayed in Brazil to rule. When Brazilian patriots demanded independence from Portugal, Pedro used it as an opportunity to further his own power. In 1822, Pedro declared Brazil an independent country and proclaimed himself emperor.

In 1889, a military revolt forced the Brazilian king to give up his throne. Brazil then became a republic. In the republic, citizens vote for their leaders in elections.

Section 2 Review

1. Why did Bolívar's dream of a unified South American nation fail to come true?

2. **Comparing and Contrasting** How was Mexico's struggle for independence different from Brazil's?

SECTION 3

Pain and Progress

What challenges did newly independent Latin American nations face?

Now that most Latin Americans were independent, they had to find ways to build their nations. In many nations, like Mexico, the army took charge of the governments.

A New Republic

After independence, Mexico struggled to form an effective government. This was a difficult task. After 11 years of war with Spain, Mexico was torn by power struggles.

Mexico also faced troubles in its territory of Texas. In the 1820s and 1830s, many people from the United States had settled in Texas. In 1835, fighting broke out between the Texans and the Mexican government. The Texans won the war. In 1836, Texas became independent.

When Texas became a part of the United States in 1845, tensions rose between the United States and Mexico. In 1846, the United States declared war on Mexico. In the war, the United States won a stunning victory. Mexico lost almost half its territory. The war also left Mexico with bitter feelings toward the United States.

Reform in Mexico

After the war with the United States, opposing groups in Mexico struggled to gain control of the government. By 1860, a group of reformers led by Benito Juárez (HWAH•rehs) won the power struggle.

Juárez became the first Native American to gain control of a country since the Spanish conquest. In 1861, Juárez was elected president of Mexico. The reformers passed laws that curbed the power of the military and of the Roman Catholic Church. They ended the special privileges of the church and seized church lands.

Juárez soon faced serious problems, however. France quickly invaded Mexico and installed an emperor. Juárez and his followers did not give up. They ousted the French and regained control of Mexico in 1867. Juárez ruled until his death in 1872.

Dictatorship and Revolution in Mexico

One of the Mexicans who led the fight against the French was the mestizo Porfirio Díaz (DEE•ahs). Díaz rose to power and ruled Mexico as a dictator from 1876 to 1911.

Two leaders of the Mexican Revolution were Pancho Villa, left, and Emiliano Zapata. Each man fought to overturn the old order in Mexico.

One day in January 1910, a short, quiet man approached Díaz. He identified himself as Francisco Madero. He told Díaz that the man Díaz had chosen for vice-president would be a very poor leader if anything should happen to Díaz.

Then the man astonished the dictator by offering himself as Díaz's next vice-president. Díaz ignored that suggestion. About a year later, Madero and a group of rebels overthrew Díaz and sent him into exile. In the first phase of the Mexican Revolution, Madero became Mexico's new president.

Madero proved unable to lead the country into bold reform. Many Mexicans wanted major changes in their country. They wanted the big estates to be broken up and the land given to villagers or small farmers.

In 1913, Madero was ousted from office and killed. General Victoriano Huerta (HWER•tah) seized power. Revolts soon broke out all over the country. Different rebel bands struggled for power. More than ten years of violence and troubles followed.

Many revolutionaries believed that the key to Mexico's future lay in economic reforms. One of the leading reformers was Emiliano Zapata (sah•PAH•tah). Zapata wanted to take land away from the wealthy. He saw the Revolution as a way to give land to poverty stricken farmers. Zapata continued to fight for change until 1919, when he was murdered by a rival.

By the time of Zapata's death, important changes were underway. There was a new constitution which included plans for land reform. Schools were set up in poor areas of Mexico and labor unions were recognized. But there would be more upheavals before the revolution was over. The Mexican Revolution did not end until the mid-1920s. Even then the promises of the revolution were left largely unfulfilled.

The changes brought about by the Mexican Revolution eventually improved the lives of Mexicans. However, the changes came at a fearful price. In the long struggle, about one million Mexicans died. This was one out of every 15 people in the country. Thousands of Mexicans fled north to the United States to escape the violence and famine.

Elsewhere in Latin America

Other Latin American countries also faced periods of trouble after they gained independence. In Argentina, for example, there was conflict between the people of Buenos Aires and the gauchos (GOW•chohs), or cowboys, of the pampas. After about 20 years of dictatorship, a democratic government gained control.

Stability and Poverty

The second half of the 1800s saw important changes taking place in Latin America. Larger countries such as Mexico, Argentina, and Chile began to make progress. Stable governments helped bring better economic times.

Latin American governments tried to attract foreign countries to invest. Latin America had tremendous natural resources. Yet, it lacked the money to develop them. Foreign countries could provide this money.

Changes in Argentina

Starting in the late 1850s, the British put a lot of money into Argentina. They built thousands of miles of railroad tracks across the grasslands. They built docks in Buenos Aires. They brought in British cattle to be raised on huge ranches.

Argentina also needed workers and began to encourage immigration. By 1914, foreigners made up about 30 percent of Argentina's population. Most immigrants came from Spain and Italy.

Foreign investment caused new problems for Latin American countries. They now depended on the industrial nations. Hard times abroad could mean economic disaster in Latin America as well.

Furthermore, the new wealth did not benefit most Latin Americans. A huge gap remained between the few wealthy people and the masses of poor people.

The End of Spanish Rule

Cuba and Puerto Rico were Spain's last colonies in the Americas. During the 1800s, they struggled to free themselves from Spain's control. The Spanish put down the rebellions with great brutality. Angered by such brutality, the United States entered the fight in 1898.

After a brief war, Spain lost its colonies. But Cuba and Puerto Rico did not gain full independence. The United States took over

On Assignment...

What struggles and challenges did Latin American countries face as they fought for and won independence? Choose some of the most action-packed events to include in your mini-history.

Puerto Rico. It also played a major role in the affairs of Cuba.

Other Latin Americans watched these developments with alarm. They worried about how far the United States might go in trying to control Latin America.

Central America

The people of Central America were especially worried. Central America was largely agricultural. Its economy depended on the export of coffee and bananas. Foreign companies, especially from the United States, were attracted by the profits to be made from these crops.

Large U.S. companies dominated Central America for many years. One company, the United Fruit Company, dominated the banana trade. It also controlled some Central American governments.

Workers resented the power of the foreign-owned companies. They believed that the United States used its influence to protect U.S.-owned businesses. In the future, these feelings would lead to unrest and revolution. You will read more about those events in Chapter 5.

Section 3 Review

1. What reforms did Benito Juárez undertake?

2. **Identifying Cause and Effect** Name one effect of foreign investment in Latin America.

I. Reviewing Vocabulary

Match each word on the left with the correct definition on the right.

1. mission
2. viceroy
3. Creole
4. peon

a. a person who governs in place of the king or queen
b. a poor person who works all his or her life for rich landowners
c. a person in Spanish Latin America whose parents or ancestors were Spanish
d. a religious settlement devoted to spreading Christianity

II. Understanding the Chapter

Answer the questions below on a separate sheet of paper.

1. How did Spain's American colonies make Spain the wealthiest nation in Europe during the 1500s?
2. What was the role of Roman Catholic missionaries among the Native Americans?
3. How did Haiti gain its independence?
4. What impact did foreign investment have on the countries of Latin America?

III. Building Skills: Summarizing

On a separate sheet of paper, write a few sentences that summarize each topic below.

1. Summarize the role of one class of people in New Spain: Africans, Creoles, mestizos, mulattos, or Native Americans.
2. Summarize Simón Bolívar's and José San Martín's roles in the struggle for Latin American independence.
3. Summarize the Mexican Revolution and how it changed Mexico.

IV. Working Together

Form a small group. With your group, create an illustrated time line showing the main events in Latin America's struggle to gain independence from Spain.

On Assignment...

Creating a Mini-History: Review the notes you and your group members took while you were reading the chapter. Together, decide on three topics to present in your mini-history. Brainstorm ideas on how to present the topics in pictures and words. Keep in mind that the audience is third graders. Plan a 10- to 12-page booklet in which to present your mini-history. Ask your classmates for feedback before preparing the final draft of your mini-history.

CHAPTER 4

Changing Patterns of Life in Latin America

How has life in Latin America changed in recent times?

The soaring lines of the new stock exchange building in Mexico City symbolize how Latin America is becoming a modernized urban society.

On Assignment...

Creating a Storyboard:

A storyboard is a plan of action in pictures. It is made up of a series of cartoons or sketches that show key scenes in a movie or television show. Filmmakers use storyboards to plan the scenes of a movie. Imagine that you have been asked to create a storyboard for a film about the people of Latin America. At three points in the chapter, there are hints to help you sketch storyboard panels for the film. At the end of the chapter, you will put your panels together and present your storyboard to the class.

Looking at Key Terms

- **dialect** a form of a language that belongs to a certain region
- **urban** characteristic of a city or city life
- **liberation theology** a belief that the Roman Catholic Church should take an active role in ending poverty in Latin America
- **chaperon** an older person who accompanies a boy and girl on a date to assure proper behavior
- **squatter** person who settles on land he or she doesn't own

SECTION 1

A Land of Many Cultures

What are the cultural roots of Latin Americans?

A newspaper writer in Ecuador goes to a party. There she meets a woman with a Native American background. She also meets a woman with Spanish ancestors. She meets a woman who speaks Quechua (kehch•WAH), a Native American language. She meets a woman who is a devout Roman Catholic. Finally, she meets a woman who observes a Native American religion.

Question: How many women has she met?

Answer: In Latin America, the writer could have met just one person!

A Blend of Cultures

As you have read, the people of Latin America have their roots in many parts of the world. Some have Native American backgrounds. Others have African, European, or Asian backgrounds.

Some Latin Americans have a background that blends two of the cultures. Some have roots in three or four cultures. The word used to describe this mix of cultures is diversity. Diversity means "differences."

Latin America is a very diverse region. However, some countries are more diverse than others. The greatest diversity is in countries such as Mexico and Brazil. Here Native American, African, and European influences have mixed since the 1500s. The least diverse countries are Argentina and Uruguay where the European influence has been strongest. Few Native Americans live in these countries. Disease and fighting nearly wiped them out during the Spanish takeover. (See Chapter 3.)

Despite the diversity, some generalizations can be made about the people of Latin America. For example, most Latin

On Assignment...

The first scene of your film could be about the cultural diversity of Latin America. Sketch out ideas for your first storyboard panel. The sketches could show the person the writer met at the party in Ecuador. One sketch might show the person explaining her traditions. Another could show her explaining her religion. Use cartoon "bubbles" to write the words.

Americans speak Spanish and most are Roman Catholic.

The Role of Culture

Culture is the way of life of a group of people. Everyone has a culture. We grow up with it. The language we speak is part of our culture, as are our religious beliefs and the foods we eat.

A culture also includes the governments that people set up and the ways in which people make a living. Culture includes music, art, and literature. In short, culture is all the things that make up a people's way of life.

Culture affects many aspects of our life. It affects what we consider right and wrong. It influences what we consider beautiful. It helps determine our goals for the future.

Section 1 Review

1. (a) What is diversity? (b) Give an example of diversity in Latin America.

2. **Applying Information** (a) What historical events account for the diversity within many Latin American nations? (b) What accounts for the lack of diversity within some others?

Daily Life in Latin America

What cultural traditions do Latin Americans have in common?

We talk of Latin America's many cultures because there is no single Latin American culture. Like the people, the cultures of Latin America blend many heritages. These blends differ from one nation to another. Daily life in Latin America reflects the mix of cultures, offering a variety of experiences.

Latin America's Many Languages Spanish is the language most Latin Americans speak. However, Brazilians speak Portuguese. In Haiti, the official language is French. In Suriname, it is Dutch. English is the official language on many Caribbean islands such as Trinidad and Tobago and Jamaica.

In addition, millions of people speak a Native American language such as Quechua or Guaraní. Some speak only a Native American language. Others speak both their Native American language and Spanish. In fact, Peru and Paraguay have two official languages. One is Spanish. In Peru the other is Quechua and in Paraguay it is Guaraní.

Across the Language Divide Language is one of the most important links for people across Latin America. For example, because most people speak Spanish, someone from Colombia could communicate with someone from Peru. Although Brazilians speak Portuguese, some can understand Spanish-speaking people.

Over the years, differences in the Spanish language have developed. In some countries, Native American words have been added to the Spanish language. Each Latin American region also has its own Spanish **dialect,** or form of the language.

The meaning of some words may differ from place to place. For example, in Cuba, "bus" is *guagua*. In Chile, it is *micro*. In Mexico, it is *camión*. Ask for a *torta* in Mexico and you will receive a sandwich. Ask for the same thing in Chile and you will be served a slice of layer cake.

Despite the minor differences in dialect, the language is the same. Therefore, most Latin Americans who speak Spanish can understand one another.

Life in Latin America is strongly affected by religious ties to the Roman Catholic Church. Here, a parade in Cuzco, Peru, blends Catholic and Native American practices.

Religion in Latin American Life

Most Latin Americans share the same religion. More than 90 percent of the people are Roman Catholic. The church continues to be an important force in Latin American life.

Everyday life is strongly affected by religion, particularly in rural areas. In tiny villages in the mountains, churches are the center of the community. Almost every home has a table decorated with statues of saints.

In general, religious ties have weakened among people who have moved to the cities from villages. In recent years, however, poor city people have strengthened their religious ties. You will read more about this trend below.

Sometimes, the people of Latin America have mixed their traditional practices with the Roman Catholic religion. Native Americans and people of African heritage who have converted to the Roman Catholic religion often blend traditional practices into their new faith.

Protestant churches have attracted large numbers of Latin Americans in recent years. Many people in **urban** areas, or cities, have converted to Protestant religions.

There are Jews, Muslims, and Hindus in Latin America. However, their numbers are small.

The Changing Role of the Catholic Church As you read in Chapter 3, the Spanish and Portuguese settlers brought the Roman Catholic religion to Latin America. In the early years, many church leaders and clergy worked to defend the rights of the weak and poor. Over time, the church grew in power and wealth. It eventually became the largest landowner in Latin America. As its wealth grew, the church more often supported the wealthy classes.

Latin Americans felt that the church was tied too closely with Latin America's rich people. Many thought the church opposed reforms that might threaten its own wealth. Such reforms included redistributing land to the poor.

In the 1960s, support grew to strip the church of some of its power. More and more, the role of the church came under attack.

In response, some Catholic leaders called for change. They demanded efforts to help the poor. They helped build clinics in the cities. They worked to provide education for the young. These actions increased the loyalty of many poor city dwellers to the church.

Liberation Theology Many priests and nuns thought these actions did not go far enough. They argued that the church had to take a more active role in ending Latin American poverty. They proposed a new idea. It came to be known as **liberation theology.** *Liberation* means "freedom." *Theology* is the study of religious belief.

Liberation theology held that poverty was created by the people who had power in society. The Catholic Church had to do more than just help the poor. It had to help change the society that created such poverty.

Thousands of priests and nuns took up liberation theology. They moved into poor urban neighborhoods. There they helped the poor organize groups to fight for change. They also formed movements to force governments to make changes in society.

Many church members opposed liberation theology. Some argued that a church should only deal with religious matters and stay out of politics. Leaders in the church ordered priests not to become political leaders. Thus, not everyone who worked for change accepted liberation theology.

Cultural Life

Another institution that plays a large role in Latin American life is the family. Most Latin Americans have a strong sense of family loyalty. Most people are supported by an extended family. This includes cousins, aunts, uncles, and other relatives. Often, several generations of a family live in one home.

"Mi Casa Es Su Casa." Most social events involve the family and the home.

Family ties are especially strong in Latin America. Here, a family in Buenos Aires, Argentina, gathers for one of the most important family ceremonies—a baptism.

Most of a child's early life is spent with members of the family. Families mark birthdays, weddings, and saints' days with major celebrations. Sometimes the parties will last all night. Guests are welcomed with the greeting *"Mi casa es su casa."* This means "My house is your house."

Family ties are especially strong in rural areas. Cousins, uncles, and aunts usually live nearby. If someone is ill, other family members are there to help.

Family ties are not as great in the cities. Newcomers often feel alone. If they have an accident or lose their jobs, there is often no one to help them.

Godparents An important Latin American tradition is that of godparents. It is considered an honor to be asked to serve as *padrino* (godfather) or *madrina* (godmother) to a child. Godparents provide young people with support as they are growing up. If a child's parents die, the godparents take on the responsibility of raising the child.

Dating In the past, young people could date only with a parent's permission. They were accompanied by a **chaperon**, an older person who ensured proper behavior. Today, however, the traditional patterns are changing. Young people now meet on their own.

Most young people live at home until they get married. When a Latin American woman marries, she does not give up her family name. If Maria García marries Eduardo Martínez, she becomes Maria García de Martínez.

All children bear a given name, the father's family name, and the mother's family name, in that order. Thus, if Maria García and Eduardo Martínez have a son whom they name Gabriel, the child's full name will be Gabriel Martínez García.

Changing Role of Women In the traditional family, the father heads the household. He is expected to support the family. The mother is responsible for raising the children and for maintaining religious ties.

In rural areas, the tradition of *machismo* remains strong. *Machismo* means "male dominance." A woman is expected to accept whatever her husband decides. Many families believe that girls do not need an education. Therefore, many girls in rural areas cannot read or write.

In rural areas, women carry the main burdens of the family. They do most of the farming. They buy and sell goods at market.

In the cities, however, many women have jobs outside the home. The money they earn often keeps the family going and at the same time gives women a sense of independence.

More women are earning university degrees and entering professions. Many women have become lawyers and doctors in recent years. Yet they often have a hard time finding jobs. This is due in part to traditional discrimination against working women.

Foods of Latin America

It is not surprising that foods in Latin America are different from place to place. However, some foods can be found in almost all countries. These include tomatoes, beans, rice, potatoes, corn, and chicken. A wide variety of fresh fruits is also available. Latin American foods usually blend Spanish and Native American or African ingredients.

Each country has its own food specialty. One of the most popular dishes in Mexico is *guacamole* (gwah•kuh•MOH•lee). It consists of avocados seasoned with hot peppers and tomatoes. In Argentina and Uruguay, the specialty is the *asado* (ah•SAH•doh), an outdoor barbecue of roasted meats. The national dish of Brazil is *feijoada* (fay•ZWAH•dah), black beans cooked with sausages, beef, and pork.

Most Latin Americans eat their main meal at midday. This meal consists of several courses. It includes soup, rice and beans, and meat or fish. Dinner is usually a simple dish or snack. It is not served until 8 or 9 p.m.

Section 2 Review

1. How does language help link the people of Latin America?
2. **Defending a Point of View** Do you think it is a good idea for young people to be accompanied by a chaperon on dates? Why or why not?

SECTION 3

A Region of Cities

What are the characteristics of Latin American cities?

La Paz is Bolivia's most important city. La Paz lies in a deep canyon on the Bolivian plains. At the base of the canyon are the large houses of the wealthy. These houses are often surrounded by high walls. Many houses have a half dozen or more bedrooms, large spaces for entertaining, and apartments for live-in servants. Nearby are high-rise buildings, shops, and offices. Climbing toward the top of the canyon are the shacks of the poor people. Many of these shacks perch on the edge of the canyon.

Until recently, there were only two classes of people in La Paz: a rich minority and a poor majority. There are still few rich and many poor in La Paz. In recent years, however, the city has changed in two major ways.

- There are many more middle class people in La Paz. Middle class neighborhoods have grown up in downtown La Paz. Government workers, merchants, and office workers all have come to live in the city. They occupy the apartment houses that are being built all over the downtown. Middle class suburbs have spread out along the canyon floor. Now they are beginning to creep up the canyon. One such middle class suburb is Villa Fatima. It is built on a steep canyon wall overlooking downtown La Paz. Here, a family may sit on a patio that is little more than a ledge in the canyon side.

- Poor people have flooded into La Paz from all over Bolivia. They have crowded into whatever free space they can find. As the poor people have entered the city, the search for living space grows harder. Many people have built homes on the steepest slopes of the canyon. Some people live in places not meant to support humans. Heavy rains cause landslides that sweep homes down into the canyons. Stone walls help keep small children from tumbling down the cliff.

Despite the hardships, people still flow into La Paz. As you will read on the following page, the city offers more opportunity than the countryside. People who move to La Paz dream of making a better life for themselves and their children.

Booming Cities

What's happening in La Paz is happening all over Latin America. Until the 1950s, most Latin Americans were farmers. Since the 1960s, huge numbers of Latin Americans have moved from rural areas to cities. Today, Latin American cities are growing by about 14 million persons a year.

People come to the cities to escape poverty. They hope to find better jobs, education for their children, and better living conditions.

About three out of every four Latin Americans now live in cities. This is one of the highest rates in the world. In Asia and Africa, about one in three people live in the cities. One in three Latin Americans lives in a city with more than a million people.

The Great Cities Latin America is the land of the "mega-city." Mega-cities are places where a large portion of the people of a country live. For example, there are 32 million people in Argentina. About 12 million, or 37.5 percent, of them live in Buenos Aires. Santiago has 5 million of Chile's 12 million people. Mexico City is home to 20 million of the 90 million people who live in Mexico.

Latin America has some of the world's fastest-growing mega-cities. For example, by the year 2000, Mexico City may have a population of more than 30 million!

More than 20 Latin American cities have populations larger than one million. Four Latin American cities are among the world's ten largest urban areas. They are Mexico City in Mexico, Rio de Janeiro and São Paulo in Brazil, and Buenos Aires in Argentina.

Many of Latin America's cities are very modern. They have towering skyscrapers and busy highways. They have mass transit rail lines and busy airports.

Parts of these cities are very attractive. There are wide streets, tall buildings, and beautiful shops and homes. They also have restaurants, theaters, and universities. Latin America's growing middle class lives in the cities. Here, children have the best chance for an education.

The Darker Side of City Life Rapid growth has made urban living difficult. Many of the largest Latin American cities have high levels of air pollution. There are few rules restricting how and where buildings may be constructed. Factories are often built close to housing areas and spew smoke into these areas.

Barrios and Slums Most cities are divided into neighborhoods called barrios. Most workers commute from their barrios to work. To get there, many workers spend two or three hours a day riding a bus. Urban highways are often jammed with traffic. During rush hours, the traffic often comes to a stop.

The poorest city people live in terrible slums. These people are usually **squatters.** Squatters are people who settle on land they do not own. Many of these squatters have low paying jobs. Others are recent arrivals from rural areas and are therefore unemployed. When they move, they do so in the middle of the night. They quickly build shacks on public land. The squatters use sheet metal, aluminum, and scraps of lumber to build their shacks.

Lima In recent years, the people of Peru have been fleeing the countryside for Lima and other cities. More than a thousand Peruvians a day come to live in Lima. "The city has grown like a wild animal," one expert has said.

In one case, 600 families took over land that had once been a garbage dump in Lima. Overnight, they built straw huts. The police moved in the next day. They threw out the families and tore down the huts. But the

On Assignment...

For your third storyboard, show life in urban Latin America. Based on the information in this section, sketch pictures that capture life in a Latin American city.

In the mountains of Bolivia, farmers prepare the land for potato planting. High up in the Andes, potatoes are one of the few crops that grow well.

settlers came back the next day. Within six months, 10,000 people were living in the former garbage dump. It had become a shantytown — a place filled with tumbledown shacks and poor people.

Crime is widespread in the shantytown. Pollution there makes people's eyes water. These days, the police rarely come to the shantytown. The people of the town have organized their own patrols. Water is brought in with barrels. No one collects trash. Residents just dump it by the side of the road.

Village Life

For Latin American peasants, life continues much as it has for centuries. Most villages have fewer than 400 people. The pace of life is slow. In warm climate regions, when the sun is hottest at midday, no one is to be seen. People stay indoors to escape the brutal heat. There may be no school in the village. If there is, children must often walk miles to get to it. Very few people can read or write. They learn about the outside world by listening to the radio or attending movies.

Landowners and Peasants Most of Latin America's cash crops are grown on large farms. These farms are usually owned by a single family. The family does not work the land. Instead, peasants pay rent to farm the owners' land.

The landowners make large profits by demanding high rents from the peasants. These rich landowners live most of the year in large cities. A manager runs the plantation for them. This system of land ownership has caused serious problems in Latin America.

Some small farmers do own land. Most often, the soil is very poor. The small farmer is too poor to buy fertilizer and good seed. In remote areas, some farmers use the same methods their ancestors used centuries ago. Other farmers survive by raising animals on hillsides. Poverty in rural areas is the main reason farmers move to cities. For many poor farmers, the city is the only hope for a better life.

Section 3 Review

1. How have Latin American cities changed in recent years?

2. **Proposing Solutions** The cities of Latin America face huge problems. Identify two of these problems and propose a possible solution to each of them.

Inside a Shantytown in Caracas

At night, when the sun goes down, the city of Caracas (kah•RAH•kahs), Venezuela, provides a show of light and sounds. The high-rise buildings sparkle. Automobile head-lights glow like fire-flies as they move slowly down the broad avenues. Fine shops stay open late, catering to wealthy shoppers. Outdoor cafes are filled with young people. The subway, called the Metro, glides through the city.

During the 1970s, Venezuela had an oil boom. Money from the sale of oil poured into Caracas. High-rise buildings and highways sprouted across the city. This created what city residents proudly called "Miami with mountains."

From Town to Shanty

From his shack on a hillside overlooking the city, Marcos Lopez Crespo can watch the city's light and sound show. Four months ago, he first came to the hillside from the village of Maturín (mah•toor•REEN) in the east. Then, he was awed by the lights. He could stand for hours watching the movement, hearing the noises.

After a while, he stopped noticing. There were too many other things to do. His cousin Hector helped Marcos. Hector had come to Caracas six years before. He knew his way around the city.

Hector and Marcos collected pieces of metal and wood from an abandoned construction site. With these, they built a one-room shack. Then, with Hector's help, Marcos got a job at a car wash.

Three weeks after coming to the hillside, Marcos was able to send for Juana (HWAH•nah), his wife of two years. Together they expanded their shack with flattened tin cans and scraps of wood. They put in a slab of paperboard they found on the hillside. The shack now has two rooms.

Hector showed Marcos how to tap into the city's power lines. This gave him light and electricity to run his most prized possession, his television set.

There is still no running water in the shack. A pipe at the bottom of the hill is the main source of water. Juana spends several hours each day carrying cans of water up the hill.

The slums of Caracas have been called some of the worst in the world. But Marcos doesn't think of the neighborhood as a slum. In fact, he doesn't think it's such a bad place.

Like Marcos and Juana, most of the people in the slum are recent arrivals to the city. Most have come from rural areas of Venezuela. There, living conditions are even worse than they are in the Caracas slum. Many were drawn to the city by the dream of high-paying jobs. When they reached the city, they found they lacked the skills to do any more than the lowest-paying work.

Are times hard in the slum on the hillside? Sure, Marcos says. But they are better than in Maturín. At least in Caracas, there are jobs.

Loss of Faith in Government

If he is going to improve himself, Marcos believes, he will have to do it on his own. Marcos doubts that he will get help from the government. "They are a bunch of rich old men," he says. "All they want to do is make themselves richer."

To survive, Marcos will have to get a better paying job. When he first got the car wash job, he thought he was earning enough money to live well. Now he is not sure. Prices continue to rise. "Medicines, flour, milk are always going up. My salary remains the same."

Marcos hasn't lost hope. He knows that his shack doesn't always have to remain a shack. "Look at Hector," he says. "Hector also began by washing cars. Now he has opened a little hardware shop at the base of the hill."

Six years ago, Hector put up a shack much like Marcos's. Since he paid no rent, he put the money into improving his house. Six years ago, Hector's house was made of cardboard. Now he lives in a two-story brick house.

Case Study Review

1. Why did Marcos come to Caracas?
2. **Understanding Points of View** Why doesn't Marcos think of his neighborhood as a bad place to live?

I. Reviewing Vocabulary

Match each word on the left with the correct definition on the right.

1. squatter
2. urban
3. dialect
4. chaperon

   a. person who accompanies a boy and girl on a date
   b. person who settles on land he or she doesn't own
   c. characteristic of a city or city life
   d. a form of a language that belongs to a certain region

II. Understanding the Chapter

Answer the questions below on a separate sheet of paper.

1. Which Latin American countries mentioned in the chapter have very diverse cultures? Which ones mentioned in the chapter do not have diverse cultures?
2. How has the role of the Roman Catholic Church in Latin America changed in recent years?
3. What is a "mega-city?" Describe why mega-cities are important to Latin America.
4. How has the city of Caracas changed in recent years?

III. Building Skills: Recognizing Cause and Effect

In each of the pairs of sentences, tell which is the cause and which is the effect.

1. **a.** Rural poverty is extreme. **b.** Millions of Latin Americans flood into cities.
2. **a.** Many Catholic clergy follow "liberation theology." **b.** The Roman Catholic Church has been criticized for not solving Latin American poverty.
3. **a.** Latin American cities grow. **b.** Extended family ties weaken.

IV. Working Together

Form a small group. With the group, write dramatic newspaper headlines about key facts you have learned in this chapter about Latin America. With other members of your class, make a bulletin board display of your headlines.

On Assignment...

Creating a Storyboard: Imagine that you are a filmmaker who is planning a film about Latin America. A storyboard will help you lay out your ideas for scenes in the film. To create your storyboard, put together the sketches you made as you read this chapter. Then write a brief narrative that links the three scenes in the storyboard together. Present your storyboard to the class, while you read your narrative to them.

CHAPTER 5

The Changing Face of Latin America

How have the governments and the economies of Latin American nations changed since independence?

Brazil's rapidly growing economy has made it one of the world's leading industrial nations. Above, cranes load goods for export on the docks of Rio de Janeiro.

On Assignment. . .

Creating a Map: After you have read this chapter, you will be asked to create a classroom resource map that shows a portion of Latin America. To prepare for your assignment, take notes about the countries, cities, and other locations that are discussed in the chapter. Look for countries that seem especially interesting to you. Pay attention to political events and economic programs in the countries of your choice. Hint boxes are located throughout the chapter to help you take notes.

Looking at Key Terms

- **land reform** a government policy that involves breaking up large estates and giving the land to peasants
- **exile** a person who lives in another country because of political disagreements
- **caudillo** a Spanish term for a military strongman
- **civilian** a citizen who does not belong to the military
- **illiterate** unable to read or write

SECTION 1

Divisions Over Land *đất*

Why has the issue of land reform caused conflict in Latin America?

Most of Latin America's wealth is based on its land. However, most of the region's problems also arise from the land. For most of its history, the people of Latin America have fought over control of the land. In many cases, heated battles between those who controlled the land and those who did not threw Latin American countries into conflict and disorder.

1) The Gap Between the Rich and the Poor

In Latin America, there were usually two major classes of people. One class was made up of a few very wealthy people. They owned much of the land, mineral deposits, and factories.

The poor people made up the second class. In Latin America the poor people were the majority. Most poor people farmed small plots of land. Others lived in urban shantytowns. There were few people in the middle class.

By the middle of the 1900s, the gap between the very wealthy and the very poor was wide. Farm workers had little hope of improving their lives. Their anger led to frequent violence. When this happened, the military stepped in.

In the 1900s, many workers began to join labor unions. Unionized workers fought for better wages and working conditions. The workers also pushed for a greater voice in the government.

2) Hard Economic Times

Just as some workers began to make gains, the world was hit with a major crisis. In the 1930s, the Great Depression crippled the economies of countries around the world.

For Latin America, worldwide depression meant disaster. Most of the countries of Latin America relied on exports to support their economies. If countries around the world could no longer afford to buy Latin American goods, Latin Americans would suffer terribly.

Economic problems caused political problems. Governments rose and fell quickly in many Latin American nations. To combat this, nations tried to gain control over their economies. Argentina, Mexico, and Brazil tried to build industries. By doing so, they hoped to depend less on money from exports.

3) Struggles for Land Reform

In the 1900s, **land reform** became a major issue. Land reform is a government policy that involves the breakup of large estates. Usually, the small pieces of land are given to peasants.

Those who supported land reform said that Latin America was poor because most peasants farmed land owned by the wealthy. They pointed in particular to Central America. In Guatemala, two (2/3) thirds of the land was in the hands of just 2 percent of the people. In Honduras, 5 percent of the people owned two thirds (2/3) of the farmland. *đất nông trại*

The landowners of Honduras and Guatemala were powerful. They fought any effort to change the system. They were supported by the United Fruit Company, which also owned huge amounts of land. (See Chapter 3.) The U.S. government backed the United Fruit Company.

In the early 1950s, a reform government came to power in Guatemala. It proposed breaking up the estates. Owners of United Fruit panicked. They asked the U.S. government to help them. The United States responded by supporting an invasion of Guatemala by Guatemalan **exiles** in 1954. An exile is someone who leaves (or is thrown out of) his or her native country — usually for political reasons. The U.S.-backed

On the barren altiplano, or high plain, a Bolivian farmer uses a wooden plow and the muscle power of oxen. Land reform requires money to help farmers buy modern tools.

invasion toppled Guatemala's reform government. Land reform efforts came to an end.

First Steps Toward Land Reform

In other parts of Latin America, land reform was more successful. The first Latin American nation to carry out land reform was Mexico. Beginning in 1917, huge estates were broken up. The land was given to Mexican peasants.

During the 1950s, Bolivia gave land to thousands of peasant families. Venezuela broke up land estates in the 1960s.

In Cuba, land reform was different. In the 1960s, Cuban leader Fidel Castro broke up large estates. However, the land did not go to individual peasants. Rather, the land was taken over by the state. Today, most Cuban farm workers work on farms for the Cuban government. You will read more about Cuba in Case Study 5 on pages 66–67.

Land Reform Today

Land ownership is still an issue in Latin America today. Most governments have passed reform programs. But they have not always been able to enforce them.

Land reform is one of the most bitterly contested issues in Latin America. The people who own large amounts of land strongly resist reform. They say that large estates are more efficient than a lot of small farms. Supporters of land reform believe that people who own their own land will farm it better. They also believe that it will help give poor farmers a stake in society.

Governments that carry out land reform programs hope to slow the flood of people into Latin America's cities. As you read in Chapter 4, cities are crowded with people from the countryside who are looking for work.

An effective land reform program is expensive. It requires a great deal of money to pay the people whose land is being taken away. It also requires training to teach peasants better ways of farming.

Latin American countries are facing the need for more land in other ways. Brazil has a huge undeveloped interior. The government of Brazil has supported the opening of new land. During the 1950s, the government decided to move its capital from Rio de Janeiro to the interior. The government hoped to attract people and businesses to this region. Brazil sponsored the construction of an entirely new capital city called Brasília. After a slow start, Brasília succeeded in bringing people to the interior.

A growing population has increased the need for land and resources. Logging companies have stripped trees away from large areas of Latin America's rain forests.

However, developing new land creates other problems. Many people worry that valuable natural resources will be destroyed. Each year, an area of forest larger than the state of Massachusetts is stripped of lumber in Brazil. As the forest is cut down, an army of landless peasants follows. These peasants occupy the free land.

The global community is concerned about the destruction of the world's forests for many reasons. One reason is that many species of animals and plants live in these forests. Destroying the forests puts species in danger of extinction. Another reason for concern is that Brazil's forests produce vast amounts of oxygen. Cutting down the Brazilian forests or any other forests may endanger the earth's oxygen supply.

On Assignment . . .

Make a list of the countries and cities mentioned in this section. Which countries are of particular interest to you? Why? How would you indicate these interesting facts on a map? For example, what kinds of things might you show on a map of Guatemala, Mexico, Cuba, or Brazil?

Section 1 Review

1. Why was the city of Brasília built?
2. **Supporting Generalizations** Find three facts to support this generalization: Most of Latin America's wealth is based on its land. However, most of the region's problems also arise from the land.

SECTION 2

Fighting Poverty

What factors have contributed to poverty in Latin America?

Poverty is Latin America's biggest problem. Thousands of farmers live on tiny plots of poor land. They are barely able to grow enough food for their families. Many cannot read and write.

All over Latin America, poor farmers have the same needs. They need more and better land, pure water, better roads, electricity, public schools, and health services.

Moving to the Urban Slums

As you read in Chapter 4, Latin Americans are becoming an urban people. Sadly, about one out of every three Latin American city dwellers lives in an urban slum. Many of these are people who have recently arrived from rural areas.

You have also read about the squatter villages. These shantytowns have different names in different countries. In Argentina, they are called *villas miserias*. In Brazil, they are known as *favelas*. In Venezuela, they are called *ranchos*. No Latin American nation has escaped them.

One way to escape from poverty is to get an education. However, getting an education is not easy. All Latin American countries require young people to attend school. But Latin American governments lack the funds to enforce this law. There are not enough schools and teachers for all the students. Even where there are schools, many young people do not attend. They must work instead to help support their families.

Population Increase

Another factor that contributes to poverty is Latin America's growing population. The population is growing so fast that it may double in 30 years. Rapid population growth makes it even harder for Latin Americans to feed, educate, and employ themselves.

Depending on One Crop

Latin America has sometimes been called a region of one-crop countries. For example, Colombia has long depended on one crop for most of its income. That crop is coffee. The countries of Central America depend upon selling bananas. Cuba depends upon sugar. If the crop is a poor one, the whole country suffers greatly.

Some Latin American countries are dependent on one natural resource such as tin, iron, or oil for most of their income. Copper makes up two thirds of Chile's exports. Tin accounts for three quarters of Bolivia's foreign sales. Venezuela relies on oil sales. Again, a sudden drop in world prices can badly hurt a country that depends on one natural resource.

On Assignment . . .

Add to the list of countries and cities you began in Section 1. Which countries depend on one crop or one natural resource? Think of symbols that could be used to show these resources on a map. For example, what symbol could you use for coffee? For copper?

Lacking a school building, these Bolivian children go to an outdoor school. Rapid population growth has put a strain on public services in Latin America.

In the last half century, many countries have made progress in building new industries. For example, Argentina, Brazil, Venezuela, and Mexico have become major industrial powers.

However, most Latin American countries find it very difficult to build new industries. These nations lack good transportation systems. They have little fuel to power machines. They also lack the trained workers to run the industries. Therefore, industry has been limited to a few small factories in the largest cities.

Natural Wealth, Hidden Resources

Latin America has enormous potential for wealth. It has a great deal of rich farmland. After the Middle East, Latin America has the world's largest oil reserves. Mexico and Venezuela have huge stores of oil.

Latin America also has large mineral reserves. Brazil and Chile have just begun to scratch the surface of their copper, iron ore, and tin supplies. Although Latin America still has huge debts and domestic problems, it may some day develop its exports and become economically powerful.

COUNTRIES OF LATIN AMERICA

COUNTRY	CAPITAL	AREA (Square miles)	POPULATION	AGRICULTURE AND INDUSTRIES
Anguilla (U.K.)	The Valley	35	8,800	salt, boat building, tourism
Argentina	Buenos Aires	1,065,189	33,900,000	oil, lead, zinc
Bahamas	Nassau	5,380	300,000	salt, tourism, rum
Barbados	Bridgetown	166	300,000	sugar, tourism, cotton, lime
Belize	Belmopan	8,867	200,000	sugar
Bolivia	La Paz/Sucre	424,165	8,200,000	tin, antimony, textiles, potatoes
Brazil	Brasília	3,286,470	155,300,000	coffee, cotton, sugar, steel
Chile	Santiago	292,257	14,000,000	copper, iodine, fish processing
Colombia	Bogotá	439,735	35,600,000	coffee, textiles, oil, gas, emeralds
Costa Rica	San José	19,575	3,200,000	coffee, bananas, gold
Cuba	Havana	44,218	11,100,000	sugar, tobacco, cobalt
Dominica	Roseau	290	100,000	bananas, tourism
Dominican Republic	Santo Domingo	18,816	7,800,000	sugar, cocoa, coffee, nickel, gold
Ecuador	Quito	109,483	10,600,000	bananas, coffee, oil
El Salvador	San Salvador	8,124	5,400,000	coffee, cotton, rubber
Falkland Islands (U.K.)	Stanley	4,700	1,900	sheep raising
French Guiana (Fr.)	Cayenne	43,740	133,376	gold, shrimp, timber
Grenada	St. George's	133	100,000	bananas, rum, nutmeg
Guadeloupe (Fr.)	Basse-Terre	660	400,000	tourism, sugar, rum, bananas
Guatemala	Guatemala City	42,042	10,300,000	coffee, oil, sugar, bananas
Guyana	Georgetown	83,000	800,000	sugar, bauxite, diamonds
Haiti	Port-au-Prince	10,579	7,000,000	coffee, sugar, bauxite
Honduras	Tegucigalpa	43,277	5,300,000	bananas, coffee, gold, silver
Jamaica	Kingston	4,232	2,500,000	sugar, coffee, rum, tourism
Mexico	Mexico City	761,604	91,800,000	cotton, oil, steel, silver, natural gas
Netherland Antilles (Neth.)	Willemstad	385	200,000	tourism, oil refining, offshore banking
Nicaragua	Managua	50,193	4,300,000	bananas, oil refining, gold
Panama	Panama City	29,208	2,500,000	bananas, oil refining, copper
Paraguay	Asunción	157,047	4,800,000	corn, cotton, iron
Peru	Lima	496,222	22,900,000	cotton, sugar, copper, lead
Puerto Rico (U.S.)	San Juan	3,435	3,522,037	coffee, plantains, manufacturing
Saint Lucia	Castries	238	100,000	bananas, tourism
Saint Vincent and the Grenadines	Kingstown	150	100,000	bananas, tourism
Suriname	Paramaribo	63,037	400,000	aluminum, rice
Trinidad and Tobago	Port of Spain	1,980	1,300,000	sugar, cocoa, oil
Uruguay	Montevideo	68,037	3,200,000	corn, wheat, meat packing
Venezuela	Caracas	352,143	21,300,000	steel, coffee, oil, iron
Virgin Islands (U.S.)	Charlotte Amalie	133	101,809	tourism, rum

Sources: *Microsoft Bookshelf '94*, Microsoft Corp.; *Information Please Almanac, 1995*, Houghton Mifflin, Boston

Latin America's oil reserves are an important part of its hidden wealth. It has the world's second largest oil reserves. Shown here is a drilling rig in the Mexican state of Chiapas.

Section 2 Review

1. Why are many Latin Americans moving from the country to the city?
2. **Analyzing** How does dependence on one crop or natural resource affect the economies of Latin American countries?

SECTION 3

Democracy's New Age

How did the trend toward democracy affect economic growth in Latin America?

Until recently, democracy had not taken hold in much of Latin America. In the 1800s, when most Latin American nations won independence, many people expected democratic rule. However, Latin Americans did not have experience with democracy. It would take time for Latin American nations to build democratic governments.

A Rocky Road to Democracy

The constitutions of most Latin American countries promised democracy. In many countries, however, democracy was not practiced. Power was in the hands of **caudillos** (kaw•DEE•yohz). *Caudillo* is a Spanish term for a military strongman. Caudillos came to power by the use of force. They ruled as dictators, often harshly. Yet they usually had widespread support. People valued the order that caudillos brought.

In recent years, rule by the military has become less popular. Economies have expanded. A new middle class has developed. In bigger countries, a large class of skilled workers has emerged. These people have protested against military rule.

In many countries, the military has been persuaded to give up power. New **civilian** governments have been formed. Civilians are ordinary citizens of a country. Democratic elections have strengthened civilian governments.

Democracy on the Rise Democracy is on the rise in Latin America. In Argentina, Uruguay, and Peru, elected governments replaced military dictatorships. Democratic governments in Venezuela and Colombia date back to the 1960s.

Democracy also took a step forward in Mexico. Since 1929, Mexico's elected government had been controlled by one party. In the 1980s, however, several opposition parties began to challenge the party in control.

Bringing Peace to Central America

Since independence, the region of Central America has been in conflict. In many countries, civil war has caused loss of lives and great destruction. Nicaragua is one of these countries. By the 1980s, it was torn by a

Democracy has recently been on the rise in Latin America. Above, a celebration is held to honor the first democratically elected president of Haiti, Jean-Bertrand Aristide.

struggle between two forces: the Sandinistas (sahn•dih•NEES•ahs) and the contras.

The Sandinistas came to power in the late 1970s after ousting a dictator of the long-ruling Somoza family. The Sandinistas were supported by the majority of Nicaraguans. However, more than 30,000 Nicaraguans had lost their lives in the fight to overthrow the Somozas. In addition, the nation's economy was almost destroyed.

At first, the United States supported the Sandinistas. In the early 1980s, however, the U.S. government accused the Sandinis-tas of helping Communist rebels in the nearby country of El Salvador. In late 1981, the United States approved a secret plan to support military actions against the Sandinista government. The U.S.-backed group was made up of former Somoza supporters and Sandinista leaders who no longer supported

the government. The U.S.-backed group was called the contras.

The struggle continued throughout the 1980s. Then, in February 1987, the president of neighboring Costa Rica took a bold step. Oscar Arias (AH•ree•ahs) put forward a peace plan.

It seemed fitting that Costa Rica should begin the peace process. Costa Rica is a successful democracy. It has a strong economy and a stable government. Arias's plan reflected the belief that peace should come from within the region.

Early in 1988, Daniel Ortega, the president of Nicaragua, agreed to peace talks. In February 1990, the Sandinista government held a national election. The Sandinistas were voted out of office. Violeta Barrios de Chamorro (chah•MOHR•oh), who represented an anti-Sandinista party, was elected

Civil war in Central America in the 1980s involved the United States. Above, U.S.-backed contra forces set up a roadblock in Nicaragua.

president. Both sides agreed to stop fighting and work to rebuild the nation.

Chamorro launched programs to reduce the size of the national army and to stop rebel contra forces. Programs to improve the economy were put into place. Nicaragua is making a slow recovery, but it remains one of the poorest countries in Latin America.

Promoting Economic Growth

In the 1990s, Latin American governments continued to promote growth. They built factories, turning out products such as automobiles. To widen the market for these goods, the governments lowered import taxes and other trade barriers with neighboring countries.

This development came at a high cost, however. Many Latin American governments borrowed heavily from banks in the United States and Europe. By the early 1980s, they had some of the world's biggest debts. They were also having trouble repaying their debts.

Mexico, for example, had counted on the sale of oil to pay its debts. Mexico was the world's fourth largest oil producer. But a slump in world oil prices sent Mexico into

a crisis. To make matters worse, terrible earthquakes struck Mexico in 1985. They caused thousands of deaths and billions of dollars worth of damage.

Changing Times

Yet by the middle of the 1990s, many Latin American countries were on the road to recovery. They were paying off their huge debts. In Mexico, in particular, industry was booming.

Many U.S. companies had set up factories in Mexico, where labor costs were cheaper than in the United States. In addition, Mexicans benefited from an agreement with the United States and Canada. This agreement was called the North American Free Trade Agreement, or NAFTA.

Under NAFTA, taxes and laws limiting trade were reduced. Goods could move freely among the three countries. Mexicans hoped the agreement would open up new markets in the United States and Canada.

The Promise of the Future

Latin America will face tremendous challenges and problems in the future. However, Latin Americans can point with pride to all they have accomplished over the years. One accomplishment is the creation of new cultures that blend European, Native American, and African traditions. In addition, Latin American nations have a wealth of untapped natural resources. The wise development of these resources makes the chances for change and growth great indeed.

Section 3 Review

1. What effect has a skilled working class had on military dictatorships in Latin America?
2. **Analyzing** Why did some of the nations of Latin America have a debt crisis in the 1980s?

Forty Years of Castro's Cuba

On January 1, 1959, Havana, the capital of Cuba, exploded in celebration. Thousands of people poured into the streets singing and chanting. Everywhere people dressed in black and red — the colors of revolution.

The Cuban people had often seen their dreams of good government go sour. Many Cuban presidents had promised reform. Most promises had never come to pass. Reform presidents often became corrupt dictators.

In 1933, a young army sergeant named Fulgencio Batista brought a new president into power. Off and on between 1933 and 1959, Batista was the real power in Cuba. At first, he held power mostly through presidents who owed their positions to him. But in 1952, Batista took power for himself. He then ruled as a dictator.

Batista had the support of the United States for most of his rule. He gained the support of U.S.-owned businesses in Cuba. These business owners knew that Batista would protect their interests. In turn, Batista helped himself to a share of the prosperity. He built up a huge fortune. However, most of the Cuban people still lived in poverty.

Batista's rule began to crumble in 1956. In that year, a young lawyer named Fidel Castro took a group of rebels into the mountains to fight Batista. (Castro had tried to bring down the Batista government several years earlier.) That attempt had failed and Castro had been jailed. Upon his release from jail, he went into exile, spending time in the United States and Mexico. (In 1956, Castro had returned to lead the rebels to victory.) His group began attacking army posts. Castro won the support of many students, business people, and church officials.) These groups believed that he would bring justice to the island. By the end of 1958, Batista had lost most of his support and decided to flee. He left the country with a large share of the national treasury.

Into Havana

Castro now left his base in the mountains. He led his forces on a march to Havana. Millions of Cubans turned out to cheer the rebels.

On January 8, 1959, Castro and his army entered Havana. The fight to get rid of Batista was over. But a new struggle had just begun. Castro set out to revolutionize the country. (He promised to eliminate poverty in Cuba.

Castro accepted communism and began tightening his control over the nation.) He looked to the Soviet Union to support his government. Castro put Cuba's economy under state control. He favored state ownership of land and businesses and seized plantations, factories, and other privately owned businesses. The government took hundreds of millions of dollars worth of property. Castro also raised taxes on foreign investors.

U.S. sugar companies controlled almost 75 percent of Cuba's farmland. They were angered when Castro raised taxes.

First Worries

By the middle of 1959, some Cubans were having second thoughts about Castro. They did not support Castro's move to communism. In the 1960s, thousands of Cubans left the islands. Most went to Miami, Florida. They hoped one day to reclaim their homeland from Castro.

Between 1959 and 1973, nearly 10 percent of Cuba's six million people left the island. In 1973, Castro limited the number of people who could leave. However, by that time, the Cuban-born population of Miami was almost 300,000.

Cuba Today

Cuba in the 1960s and Cuba today are very different countries. In the 1960s, about half the people lived in the countryside. By the 1990s, about 70 percent lived in cities. In 1965, about one of every three Cuban workers worked in agriculture. Today, that figure is closer to one in five.

Cuba has made great strides in providing housing, medical care, and education for its citizens. For example, better health care has resulted in a dramatic decline in the rate of infant mortality. This is the rate at which babies die in their first year of life.

Before the revolution, about half of Cuban children did not attend school. Today, many more children attend school. Only 3 percent of the population is **illiterate.** Illiterate people cannot read or write. Cuba has one of the lowest illiteracy rates in Latin America.

Yet the changes have come at a great cost. Castro rules as a dictator. With a small handful of supporters, he makes all major decisions. The Communist party is the only legal political party. There is no right to a free press. Many political prisoners are held in jail without trial.

Despite Castro's programs, Cuba is a very poor country. When the Soviet Union collapsed in 1991, Castro lost the aid that kept his economy working. Yet Castro vowed that communism would stay in place in Cuba. Whether he will be able to keep that promise remains a major question.

Case Study Review

1. Who was Fulgencio Batista? What happened to him in 1958?
2. **Drawing Conclusions** Why did many Cubans leave their country in the 1960s and 1970s?

I. Reviewing Vocabulary

Match each word on the left with the correct definition on the right.

1. exile
2. illiterate
3. civilian
4. caudillo

    a. unable to read or write
    b. citizen who does not belong to the military
    c. Spanish term for a military strongman
    d. person who leaves his or her homeland because of political disagreements

II. Understanding the Chapter

Answer the questions below on a separate sheet of paper.

1. Why did land reform efforts proceed so slowly in Latin America?
2. What was the attitude of the U.S. government toward land reform in Guatemala in the 1950s?
3. How does dependence on one crop or resource affect the economy of some Latin American countries?
4. How did the collapse of the Soviet Union in 1991 affect Cuba?

III. Building Skills: Comparing Map Projections

Our view of the world depends on the kind of map projection we use to show that world. A map projection is a way of showing the curved earth on a flat surface. On the left is a Mercator projection of the world. On the right is a Peters projection. Study the two maps and then answer the questions on page 69.

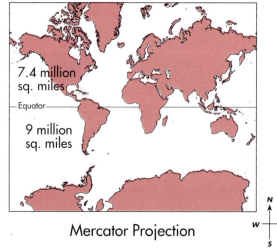

7.4 million sq. miles

Equator

9 million sq. miles

Mercator Projection

7.4 million sq. miles

Equator

9 million sq. miles

Peters Projection

N
W   E
S

1. Which map shows the Southern Hemisphere as larger, the Mercator projection or the Peters projection?
2. North America is 7.4 million square miles in area. South America is 9 million square miles in area. Which map projection shows South America as larger than North America?
3. How do you think these two maps affect the way we think of North and South America?

IV. Working Together

Form a small group. Together, write an editorial for a newspaper that supports or opposes land reform in Latin America. Find as many facts as you can in the chapter to support your point of view.

On Assignment...

Creating a Map: Review the notes you have taken as you read this chapter. Now prepare a resource map of one country that you found interesting. A resource map shows the natural resources and industries found in a particular area. First make a rough map of your country. Then mark the map with the information you collected as you read the chapter. Create a key to show natural resources and other information. Use the chart on page 62 to help you. Present your finished map to your classmates.

Latin America and the World

What role does Latin America play in the world today?

The flags of the United States and the Commonwealth of Puerto Rico fly over the fortress of El Morro in San Juan. Puerto Rico became a commonwealth of the United States on July 25, 1952.

On Assignment . . .

Creating an Illustrated Time Line: After you have read this chapter, you will create an illustrated time line of the events covered in the chapter. You will list at least ten events from the chapter in chronological order. *Chronological* means "in the order that events happened." Then you will draw pictures to illustrate at least three of those events. Take notes as you read to help you remember and organize the events.

Looking at Key Terms

- **commonwealth** a self-governing state with close ties to another more powerful state
- **gunboat diplomacy** a foreign policy that calls for threatening the use of military force to achieve a country's goals
- **tariff** a tax on goods entering or leaving a country
- **extract** to remove or take from
- **mural** a very large painting or photograph that is applied to a wall or ceiling

Latin America and the United States

Why has the relationship between Latin America and the United States often been strained?

In 1898, a fleet of U.S. ships approached San Juan Bay in Puerto Rico. Three months earlier, the United States had declared war on Spain. After a quick victory in Cuba, U.S. forces wanted to take over Puerto Rico. As the ships drew closer, the great fortress El Morro came into view. Rising 140 feet (43 meters) above the ocean, El Morro stood strong against U.S. gunfire.

This was not the first time that El Morro had been attacked. During the 1500s, British ships had tried to take the fort. In the 1600s, Dutch ships attacked it. Both forces were driven back. For nearly 400 years, Spain's flag had flown over El Morro.

As you read in Chapter 3, Spain's rule over Puerto Rico ended as a result of the Spanish-American War. On July 25, 1898, the Spanish flag was removed from El Morro. But the Puerto Rican flag did not go up. Instead, the U.S. flag was raised. Puerto Rico had become a colony of the United States.

Becoming a Commonwealth

Exactly 54 years later to the day, on July 25, 1952, another turning point in Puerto Rican history occurred at El Morro. Governor Luis Muñoz Marín (MUN•yoz mah•REEN) raised the Puerto Rican flag next to the U.S. flag at El Morro. Puerto Rico had become a **commonwealth** of the United States. A commonwealth is a self-governing state with close ties to another more powerful state. Puerto Rico now governed itself. Yet it had close ties to the United States. (See Case Study 6.)

The struggles at El Morro remind us that Latin America is not an isolated region. It is a region with strong ties to the rest of the world. In particular, Latin America has had to deal with the United States. Often, these dealings have led to anger, distrust, and even bloodshed.

Latin America and the United States have a special relationship. They share a common past as European colonies. However, most Latin Americans see the relationship as unequal. They believe that the United States has long had the upper hand in the relationship.

According to the Mexican poet Octavio Paz, the people of the United States

> *are always among us even when they ignore us or turn their back on us. Their shadow covers the whole hemisphere. It is the shadow of a giant.*

The Monroe Doctrine

Like most giants, the United States has often demanded that it get its own way. In the early 1800s, Spain lost most of its American colonies. The U.S. government worried that Spain or other European countries might try to regain control of the newly independent nations. U.S. President James Monroe feared that this would put the United States in danger.

With this in mind, Monroe issued a warning in 1823. He warned the European powers not to meddle in the Americas. Monroe stated that the United States would defend the new countries of Latin America. This statement became known as the Monroe Doctrine.

The Mexican War

In 1836, Texas won its independence from Mexico. For the next nine years, Texas remained independent. However, in 1845, it joined the United States. The Mexican people were outraged. The next year the United States and Mexico went to war over the boundary between Texas and Mexico.

Although the Mexicans fought hard, victory went to the United States. As a result of the war, the United States gained a huge area. (See Chapter 3.) Many Latin Americans thought that the United States had picked on its smaller neighbor. The bad feelings caused by the war lasted for many years.

The Spanish-American War

As you read in Chapter 3, by the mid-1800s, Spain's only colonies in Latin America were Cuba and Puerto Rico. For years, Cuba and Puerto Rico had struggled to free themselves from Spanish control. People in the United States were disturbed by newspaper stories of Spanish cruelty and sided with the colonies.

In 1898, the United States went to war with Spain. After the brief Spanish-American War, Spain lost its colonies. But Cuba and Puerto Rico did not gain full independence. The United States took over Puerto Rico. It dominated Cuba. These actions angered people on both islands. Other Latin Americans watched these developments with alarm. They worried about how much further the United States would go.

"Policing" the Americas

The United States was determined to show its muscle in Latin America. In 1902, U.S. President Theodore Roosevelt sent warships to Venezuela. Venezuela owed money to a number of European countries. Roosevelt did not want the Europeans to send troops to Latin America. He announced that the United States would act as a police force in the Americas. It would step in if Latin American countries could not pay their debts to other nations.

In 1905, Roosevelt sent troops to the Dominican Republic to make sure that the nation paid its debts. Later, U.S. Marines were sent to other Latin American countries. In each of these countries, the United States trained special armies. The commanders of these armies often seized power as military dictators.

The Panama Canal

As the United States became a world trading power, it looked for a quicker way for ships to travel between the Atlantic and Pacific oceans. The only route was a long trip around the southern tip of South America. A canal across narrow Panama would cut the Atlantic-to-Pacific voyage in half.

At that time, Panama was a territory of the country of Colombia. President Theodore Roosevelt offered to pay Colombia for the right to build a canal through this territory. When Colombia turned down the offer, Roosevelt took action to get the canal built.

In 1903, the United States encouraged Panama to stage a revolution. A U.S. warship was stationed nearby. When the revolution broke out, the warship was available to keep Colombian troops from ending the revolt.

Panama became a free country. A few weeks later, it signed a treaty with the United States. The United States won control of a strip of land called the Canal Zone.

President Theodore Roosevelt had said that when dealing with Latin America, the United States should "speak softly and carry a big stick." This cartoon reflects U.S. policy of acting as a police force in the Americas.

Building the Panama Canal in the early years of this century was a major feat. More than 35,000 workers toiled for years, cutting through mountains and clearing swamps.

Critics charged that the United States had used **gunboat diplomacy**, or military action, to gain access to the Canal Zone. This drew strong protests from Latin American countries.

The Good Neighbor Policy

In 1913, the Argentine author Manuel Ugarte (oo•GAHR•teh) wrote a critical letter to U.S. President Woodrow Wilson. Ugarte asked that "the stars and stripes cease to be a symbol of oppression in the New World." *Oppression* means "unjust use of power." Still, Wilson sent U.S. Marines to Haiti and the Dominican Republic. He also ordered two invasions of Mexico.

Twenty years later, U.S. President Franklin Roosevelt helped to better relations between Latin America and the United States. In 1933, he announced a new policy toward Latin America known as the "Good Neighbor Policy." The United States promised to respect the rights of Latin Americans. The United States agreed not to interfere in the affairs of other countries.

During World War II, a spirit of cooperation grew. The nations of the Americas worked together to defeat their enemies. By the end of the war, the United States had become the most powerful nation in the world. Latin Americans hoped that the United States would use its power and wealth to help them solve their problems.

Section 1 Review

1. What was the Monroe Doctrine?
2. **Understanding Points of View** Why did the United States send troops into Latin American countries during the early years of the 1900s?

SECTION 2

A Changing World

In what ways is Latin America's role in the world changing?

In 1959, relations between the United States and Latin America entered a new phase. In that year, Fidel Castro took power in Cuba. (See Chapter 5.) Castro denied that the United States had special privileges in the Western Hemisphere. He built up close relations with the Soviet Union and other Communist countries. He supported groups in Latin America that were trying to overthrow U.S.-backed governments.

The United States responded in different ways. One way was to support an invasion of Cuba in 1961 by anti-Castro Cubans. The United States sponsored an invasion force of

1,800 Cuban rebels that landed in Cuba at a place called the Bay of Pigs. In a matter of days, Castro's forces captured or killed most of the rebels. The failed invasion embarrassed the United States.

Since then, the United States sought other ways to oust Castro. But Castro remained in tight control of Cuba.

In the 1990s, the Soviet Union crumbled. Its economic aid to Cuba ended. This hurt the Cuban economy. It put pressure on Castro to ease Communist rule. However, Castro vowed never to accept capitalism.

Alliance for Progress

Fidel Castro was very popular in many parts of Latin America. Part of the reason was that Latin America continued to distrust the United States.

One of U.S. President John F. Kennedy's main goals was to build greater trust. In 1961, he announced a new policy known as the Alliance for Progress. The United States promised to give money to improve conditions in Latin America.

The Alliance started many useful programs. Teams carved roads out of the mountains. Banks made loans to poor farmers to buy seed. Medical teams traveled to isolated villages to care for sick people.

Still, the Alliance did not do all that Latin Americans hoped it would. The money was not always used to help the poor. Some of the money was used to keep unpopular governments in power.

Support With a Price Tag

Democracy faced a rocky road in Latin America. The United States often made choices that hurt democracy. Would it support governments with socialist or communist leanings? Or would it support military rulers who promised to protect U.S. interests? The United States often chose those who would protect U.S. interests.

In 1970, the people of Chile elected Salvador Allende (ah•YEN•deh) as president. Allende seized many businesses. He maintained warm relations with Cuba.

In 1973, the Chilean military moved against Allende. He was killed. A military dictatorship took control of Chile. It soon became clear that the United States had helped in Allende's overthrow. Many Latin Americans protested. To them, it was another example of U.S. interference in their affairs.

Opposing the Sandinistas in Nicaragua

The United States has long exercised great power in Central America. We have seen in Chapter 5 how the United States helped oust a leftist government in Guatemala in the 1950s. In 1979, leftist rebels in Nicaragua overthrew a brutal dictatorship. These rebels called themselves Sandinistas.

The Sandinistas soon showed their dislike for the United States. Then fighting broke out in Nicaragua. The United States sent aid to groups fighting the Sandinistas. It also banned all trade between Nicaragua and the United States. These events brought Nicaragua close to collapse. To end the war, the Sandinistas had to allow a free election. To their surprise, they lost the election. In early 1990, Violeta Barrios de Chamorro, an anti-Sandinista candidate, was elected president. (See Chapter 5.)

Panama Canal Update

In 1978, the United States took a major step in solving one of the big issues that angered people in Latin America. It agreed to give up control of the Panama Canal. The people of Panama were pleased. They believed strongly that a foreign nation should not control territory within their country.

Supporting Democracy in Haiti

In September 1991, the first democratically elected president of Haiti, Jean-Bertrand Aristide, was overthrown by the Haitian military. Aristide was a Roman Catholic priest who was popular with Haiti's poor. The United States reacted angrily. It banned all trade with Haiti. Haiti's economy was hurt. But the generals refused to surrender. It took the threat of invasion to force the military to give up power. In October 1994, President Aristide returned to power.

In February 1996, Haiti held elections for president. Aristide was prevented by Haitian law to run for a consecutive term. He supported candidate Rene Preval, a well-known champion of democracy. Preval won the election and became president. This marked the first peaceful transfer of power in Haiti since it declared independence in 1804.

Section 2 Review

1. How did the United States react to Fidel Castro's policies?
2. **Summarizing** Summarize how the role of the United States has changed in Latin America in the last century.

SECTION 3

Working Together

How have Latin American nations tried to build unity in the region?

For many years, Latin Americans talked about forming a union that would include all the countries of the Americas. They felt that such a union would allow them to do some things together that no one country could do alone.

exaggerated

Latin American liberator Símon Bolívar had dreamed of a united Spanish America. He wanted to unite all the new Latin American nations under one government. But the nations could not agree. Rivalries blocked all attempts at cooperation. Before his death in 1830, Bolívar wrote bitterly: "America is ungovernable. Those who have served the revolution have plowed the sea."

Bolívar's dream of bringing Latin American nations together did not die. In 1889, the nations of the Americas formed the Pan-American Union. *Pan* is a Greek word meaning "all." This group was set up to deal with common problems of the region.

In 1948, this Union grew into the Organization of American States (OAS). Member nations have worked for the peaceful settlement of disputes in the Americas.

The OAS has handled many conflicts in the Americas. It cannot force any nation to do as it says. But it can try to be a peacemaker when there is trouble.

Many Latin Americans are not satisfied with the OAS. They feel that the United States uses the organization to protect its own interests. Over the years, there have been attempts to set up another group that does not include the United States. However, none of these efforts has been successful.

In Search of Unity

Despite their differences, the nations of Latin America have reached agreement on a number of important issues. For example, they have agreed to use peaceful means to solve disputes. They have also agreed not to get involved in the internal, or national, affairs of other countries.

Encouraging Trade

Latin American countries have worked among themselves to improve their economies. One problem was the high **tariffs,** or taxes, on goods traded among Latin American countries. In 1960, Mexico and

The huge Apui trees of the Amazonian rain forest are just one of the treasures that concerned people around the world are working to preserve.

many South American countries set up an organization to reduce tariffs. In 1963, several Central American nations set up the Central American Common Market. Both these groups have helped increase trade between countries. This has helped the growth of industries within Latin America.

Saving the Rain Forest

Scientists know that effective medicines can be **extracted**, or taken, from plants in the rain forests. Yet rain forests around the world are rapidly disappearing.

Much of the battle over the disappearing rain forests centers on the Amazon basin. The Amazonian rain forest covers an area about half the size of the United States. About 90 percent of it is located in Brazil. In the 1970s, Brazil's leaders began a program to bring settlers to the Amazon region. (See Chapter 27.) The Brazilians saw forest clearing as a quick way to provide more land and a better life for their people.

The rain forest of the Amazon contains thousands of different types of plants. It has thousands of different types of animals. Some of the plants and animals found in the rain forest are valuable to humans. Curare (kyoo•RAH•ray) is an important medicine that comes from trees in the rain forest. Rubber is another useful product. It is collected from trees in the rain forest.

Efforts to save the rain forest must balance different interests. On the one hand are the people who live in the region. On the other hand are the interests of the world as a whole. Many Latin Americans believe that their economies cannot expand unless they use their untapped resources. Environmentalists, however, point out that the destruction of the rain forests affects the health and well-being of the earth.

Section 3 Review

1. What does the Organization of American States do?

2. **Understanding Points of View** Write a paragraph defending the point of view of environmentalists who wish to preserve the rain forests. Then write a paragraph defending people who wish to use the resources of the rain forests to boost their country's economy.

SECTION 4

Latin America's Cultural Contributions

What forces have influenced some of Latin America's writers and artists?

We can learn much about Latin America from its writers and artists. Many Latin American artists portray a world where nothing is secure. In this world, force rules.

Civil war happens all the time. Natural disasters disturb life. There is a vast gap between rich and poor.

García Márquez, Giant of Literature

In the past 25 years, many Latin American writers have become popular throughout the world. Perhaps the most popular author is Gabriel García Márquez. He was born in Colombia in 1928. García Márquez was one of the 16 children of a poor telegraph operator. He grew up listening to tales of civil war and ghosts. He wrote about this in his great novel *One Hundred Years of Solitude*. It traces the lives of a fictional Colombian family over a period of 100 years.

The work of García Márquez mixes dreams with reality. Dead husbands return as ghosts to frighten their wives. People fly off into the darkness. Women live on a diet of dirt. It rains for four years!

García Márquez has won worldwide fame. In 1982, he received the Nobel Prize for literature.

The "Big Three" of Mexican Art

Trains back from the battlefield unloaded their cargoes. The wounded soldiers suffered on their stretchers. In the world of politics, it was the same. It was war without quarter [mercy].

This quote from the Mexican artist José Orozco (oh•ROHS•koh) helps explain how the Mexican Revolution influenced his art. Orozco was an artist during the revolution. Two other great artists of the period were Diego Rivera and David Siqueiros (see•keh•EE•rohs). The three became Mexico's most famous artists.

They developed a truly Mexican style of art. They used the **mural**, an art form that dates back to Aztec times. A mural is a large

Mexican artists created large murals to show dramatic scenes from the history of Mexico. This mural by David Siqueiros shows a soldier during the Mexican Revolution.

picture painted on a wall. The murals of these artists used powerful images to show the history of Mexico. The murals supported the causes of the poor.

After the revolution, the three painted murals on a number of public buildings. These murals can be seen in Mexico today. Through the murals, the ideas of these artists still reach the people of Mexico.

Frida Kahlo Frida Kahlo is another well-known Mexican artist. Like those of the "big three," her paintings were infused with elements of her Mexican heritage. She worked during the 1930s and 1940s to create a number of highly personal self-portraits among other works. Kahlo was married to Diego Rivera.

Section 4 Review

1. Who is Gabriel García Márquez and what does he write about?
2. **Analyzing** How did the paintings of Mexico's "big three" artists reflect the history of their country?

Puerto Rico: An Island Commonwealth

In the autumn of 1949, Verania Gonzáles boarded a plane bound for New York. As the plane cut through the clouds, the 17-year-old from San Juan, Puerto Rico, wondered what her new life would be like. She spoke only Spanish. Her sister lived in the South Bronx, a section of New York City. Here Verania would live.

After landing, Verania caught her first glimpse of the South Bronx. She spotted Spanish signs in the windows of bodegas, small grocery stores. She heard the sounds of Spanish in the streets. Then she met Luis Cancel (kahn•SEHL). He was also 17 years old and of Puerto Rican descent. Unlike Verania, he had been born in New York.

In 1952, the couple married and took up life in the South Bronx. There the Puerto Rican population was booming. As both Puerto Ricans and New Yorkers, Luis and Verania lived through a time of many changes in their native land.

A month after the Cancels married, Puerto Rico became a commonwealth of the United States. Under the law, Puerto Ricans could elect their own officials. Puerto Ricans remained U.S. citizens. They could be drafted into the military. However, they did not have to pay federal income taxes if they lived in Puerto Rico.

The person most responsible for commonwealth status was Luis Muñoz Marín. Governor Muñoz Marín hoped to build a sense of pride among the people of his island. He created a program known as Operation Bootstrap. It was designed to improve the economy and the standard of living of Puerto Ricans. Puerto Ricans were asked to "pull themselves up by their own bootstraps."

A Drive to Modernize

To provide jobs, Muñoz Marín invited U.S. companies to build factories in Puerto Rico. Through foreign investment, Muñoz Marín hoped to change Puerto Rico into a modern industrial society.

Operation Bootstrap brought great changes to the island. In 1952, there were only 82 factories in all of Puerto Rico. By 1970, the island had more than 1,000 factories. Thousands of new jobs were created.

Workers moved into new public housing. New paved roads crisscrossed the island. The literacy rate soared.

Despite these advances, there is growing debate over Puerto Rico's status. An independence movement has formed. Independistas call for an end to all political ties with the United States. They believe that independence is best for the future of Puerto Rico.

On the other side are people who want Puerto Rico to become a state of the United States. They especially want the right to be represented in the U.S. Congress.

For most Puerto Ricans, the island's political status remains a very important issue. Few Puerto Ricans support independence. Most favor ties with the United States. But just what will these ties be? Will Puerto Rico continue to be a commonwealth? Or will it become a state?

On Assignment. . .

Conclude your list of the events in this chapter for which dates have been given. Which dates are most important? Why? Think of images to accompany the important dates.

Case Study Review

1. What is Puerto Rico's relationship with the United States today?

2. **Determining Cause and Effect** Identify one short-term and one long-term effect of Puerto Rico's commonwealth status.

Under Operation Bootstrap, Governor Luis Muñoz Marín invited U.S. companies to build factories and plants in Puerto Rico. This electronics factory was built during the 1970s.

I. Reviewing Vocabulary

Match each word on the left with the correct definition on the right.

1. gunboat diplomacy
2. extract
3. commonwealth
4. tariff

    a. a self-governing state with close ties to another more powerful state
    b. threatened use of force to achieve foreign policy goals
    c. tax on goods entering or leaving a country
    d. to remove or take from

II. Understanding the Chapter

Answer the questions below on a separate sheet of paper.

1. How did the "Good Neighbor Policy" attempt to change U.S. policy toward Latin America?
2. How did the U.S. policy supporting Haiti's president Aristide differ from its policy toward Chile's president Allende in the 1970s?
3. What goals did the Alliance for Progress have?
4. What was "Operation Bootstrap"?

III. Building Skills: Reading a Chart

Read the chart and answer the questions on page 81.

U.S. Investment in Latin America, 1987–1914 (in millions of dollars)

	Caribbean	Mexico and Central America	South America	Total
1897	4.5	221.4	37.9	263.8
1908	220.2	713.0	129.7	1,062.9
1914	329.0	946.7	365.7	1,641.4

1. What happened to U.S. investments in Latin America during the period of 1897–1914?

2. Did U.S. investments in Latin America grow faster in 1897–1908 or in 1908–1914?

IV. Working Together

Latin America is a diverse place. Its countries have many different types of governments. With a small group of classmates, pick one country of Latin America. Find out what kind of government that country has today. Find out about its experience with democracy. In addition, find out about U.S. relations with that country. Report your findings to the class.

On Assignment...

Creating an Illustrated Time Line: Put together the list of events you have collected for your time line. Pick out the ten events that you think are the most important. Then create a time line that shows these events in the order in which they happened. Pick three of the events from your time line and draw pictures of each of them.

CHAPTER 7

Canada: Building the Mosaic

What challenges does Canada face as a culturally diverse nation?

Founded in 1608, the city of Quebec has a distinct French Canadian flavor. French Canadians have a strong sense of identity that sets them apart from other Canadians.

On Assignment. . .

Making a Presentation: Imagine that you work for the Canadian Department of Tourism. You have been given the job of preparing a three-minute talk about Canada to tourists. In your presentation, you are to describe Canada's geography and people. As you read this chapter, look for On Assignment hint boxes to help you make notes for your talk. At the end of the chapter, you will write your talk and present it.

Looking at Key Terms

- **mosaic** a design made up of many small pieces of materials
- **province** a territory governed as an administrative or political unit of a country
- **hydroelectricity** the power that comes from the force of rushing water
- **bilingualism** the policy of recognizing two official languages
- **Commonwealth of Nations** the group of nations that were once colonies of Great Britain
- **federal system** a system in which power is divided between a central government and a local government

The Land of Canada

How does geography make it hard for Canada to be a united nation?

"Let Canada be free!"

Those stirring words were uttered in 1774. In those days, the British Empire had just taken over France's empire in North America. French-speaking people made their feelings clear. They did not want to be part of Britain's 13 colonies to the south. They wanted to maintain their language, laws, and culture.

More than 200 years later, a similar cry is being heard in Canada. It has raised concerns that this huge country to the north of the United States may break up.

By sheer size alone, Canada demands attention. From coast to coast, it stretches out over 4,500 miles (7,200 km). Canada is the world's second largest country, ranking just after Russia.

Canada possesses vast wealth in natural resources. These natural resources fuel several large industries that contribute to the country's strong economy. Canadians enjoy one of the highest standards of living in the world.

Unfortunately, Canada's huge size divides Canadians. Canadians tend to live in pockets of settlements scattered across the country. Each pocket is separated from the others by geographic barriers. The people around Ontario, for example, are separated from the people of the prairies by hundreds of miles of forests and lakes. The Rocky Mountains separate the people of British Columbia from the prairies. (See the map on page 85.)

Although railroads and airplanes have helped break down these barriers, Canadians still tend to have a strong sense of loyalty to the region in which they live. Sometimes this regional loyalty is stronger than national loyalty.

Canadians often speak of their nation as a **mosaic**. A mosaic is a design made up of many small pieces of materials. From a distance, those pieces blend into one picture. But as you move closer, you become aware of the role each of the separate pieces plays in the overall design.

Canada's Provinces

Take a look at the map on page 85. As you can see, Canada is divided into **provinces** and territories. A province is an area or region that is part of a larger country. The powers of government are divided between the provincial governments and Canada's national government.

Canada is made up of ten provinces. From east to west, the provinces are Newfoundland, Prince Edward Island, Nova Scotia, New Brunswick, Quebec (kuh•BEHC), Ontario, Manitoba, Saskatchewan (seh•SKACH•eh•wahn), Alberta, and British Columbia. There are also two territories — the Yukon and the Northwest Territories.

Nunavut At the beginning of the 21st century, a third territory will be carved from the central and eastern portions of the Northwest Territories. This territory will be called Nunavut, which means "Our Land" in the Inuit (IN•yoo•it) language. The Inuit are a culture group who live in the cold Arctic north.

The territory of Nunavut is about 772,000 square miles (2 million sq. km) — about one fifth of Canada's territory. It includes Baffin and Ellesmere islands. Baffin Island is Canada's largest island. Most of the 21,000 people in Nunavut are Inuit. An agreement made with the Canadian government in 1992 allows the Inuit to gain control over the territorial government and to control hunting and fishing rights by 1999.

Canada's Geographic Regions

Canada can be organized into six major geographic regions: the Maritime Provinces, the St. Lawrence and southern Ontario lowlands, the Canadian Shield, the Central

Canada's Maritime Provinces have a close connection with the sea. Most people make their living through fishing or seafaring. Here, a lighthouse towers over the rocky Atlantic coast of Nova Scotia.

Plains, the Western Mountain region, and the Arctic North. The history, geography, and people combine to give each region a distinct character.

Maritime Provinces East of the St. Lawrence River lie the Maritime provinces. The Maritimes are sometimes called the Atlantic provinces. The provinces that make up this region are Newfoundland, Nova Scotia, New Brunswick, and Prince Edward Island.

The Maritimes have a close connection with the sea. Many people of the Maritimes earn their living through fishing and seafaring. In recent times, however, the waters have been overfished and stocks of fish have been declining. This has thrown the fishing industry of the Maritimes into crisis. The people of the Maritimes hope that recent discoveries of offshore oil and natural gas will boost the region's economy.

The Lowlands The St. Lawrence and southern Ontario lowlands lie further south and west along the St. Lawrence River and the Great Lakes. This region falls across the southern portion of Quebec and Ontario. A moderate climate, fertile farmland, and access to good water routes attracted many settlers to the region in the 1700s and 1800s. Today the lowlands contain 60 percent of Canada's entire population, making it the most populated area of the country.

The St. Lawrence Seaway has much to do with the economic success of the lowlands. Opened in 1959, this joint Canadian and U.S. project built a series of locks along the St. Lawrence River. The locks allow large ocean liners to sail from the Atlantic Ocean, along the St. Lawrence River, and into Lake Ontario. Every year several million tons of goods are transported through the seaway.

Canada's largest cities are located in the lowlands. These cities include Toronto, Montreal, and Quebec. Ottawa, the federal capital of Canada, is also located in the lowlands.

Canadian Shield North and west of the lowlands is a massive rock formation. It is known as the Canadian Shield. The Shield is a treasure house of minerals. It has hundreds of thousands of square miles of forests. It also has thousands of lakes. The lakes were formed by giant sheets of ice called glaciers that melted thousands of years ago.

In fact, Canada has more lakes than all the rest of the world combined. There are so many lakes that some of them do not even have names.

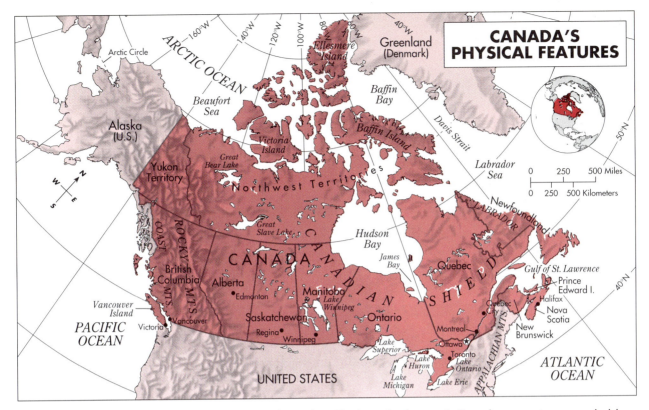

CANADA'S PHYSICAL FEATURES

Location From Newfoundland in the east to the Yukon Territory in the west, Canada presents a remarkable array of physical wonders. What island lies furthest east? What island is its northernmost point?

Central Plains The Central Plains are located west of the Canadian Shield and east of the Rocky Mountains. These rolling plains stretch across North America from the Gulf of Mexico to the Arctic Ocean. This region contains some of the world's richest farmland. Because massive amounts of wheat grow here, it is known as the "bread-basket" of Canada.

Western Mountains Western Canada is marked by great mountain ranges. Before the days of air travel, the Rocky Mountains formed a huge barrier between eastern and western Canada. Few mountain passes make the Canadian Rockies difficult to cross.

West of the Rockies lie the Coastal Ranges. These mountains are lower, but still difficult to cross. Most people in this region live in a small flat coastal area in the Fraser valley. Vancouver, the region's chief city, is located at the mouth of the Fraser River.

Arctic North The region of Canada that lies farthest to the north is the Arctic. This is a region of ice and snow. The Yukon, Northwest, and soon-to-be-formed Nunavut territories are located in the Arctic North. Few people live in this vast, cold region. The Inuit have survived in the Arctic by hunting and fishing. Other culture groups in the territories include the Dene and the Métis. You will read more about the Métis in Section 3.

On Assignment...

What would you tell visitors to Canada about its physical regions? To which regions would you recommend tourists go? Why?

Thousands of years ago, giant glaciers gouged huge chunks of rocks and earth out of the landscape. The result: lakes, thousands of them, such as beautiful Lake Moraine in the Canadian Rockies.

Canada's Climates

Any country as large as Canada is bound to have a variety of climates. Canada reaches north almost to the North Pole. However, the southern tip of Ontario province is almost the same latitude as northern California. Latitude is a measure of distance north or south of the equator.

Despite the variety, a few generalizations may be made about Canada's climate. Generally, winters are long and cold. Cold winds blow south from the Arctic. They bring frigid weather for much of winter. Sometimes the temperature gets as low as 80 degrees below zero. Further south, in the prairies, it is not as cold. However, it is cold enough so that winter blizzards are a familiar part of life. Summers are short.

On the west coast, the climate is far different. Warm, moist air blows in from the Pacific. This gives coastal regions a mild climate year round.

Resources

Canada's supply of natural resources is huge. Vast forests support a thriving lumber industry. Canada is the world's leading producer of paper. The rich soil of the prairies makes Canada one of the world's leading growers of wheat. Canada also has valuable stores of oil and iron ore. Canada's rushing rivers are a source of electric power.

Section 1 Review

1. How has Canada's size kept its people divided?

2. **Expressing an Opinion** The people of Canada often feel more loyal to their region than to the nation as a whole. In your opinion, what are some of the things that unify a nation? What are some of the things that divide a nation?

Canada's Native Americans

Who were the first Canadians?

Scientists believe that the first people to arrive in North America came from Asia. About 30,000 years ago, people traveled over a land bridge that connected North America and western Asia. As you read in Chapter 2, this land bridge was exposed during the last ice age. The people who crossed the bridge fanned out in all directions. Some people went south, while others went east. Those who went east became the first humans to live in what today is Canada. These people are often called Native Americans.

Groups of Native Americans traveled across the continent. Each group developed its own distinct culture. However, one thing all the groups had in common was respect for the earth. Native Americans viewed the earth as a provider of food and shelter for all living creatures. Each group of Native Americans developed rituals and ceremonies to honor the environment. Each generation taught the rituals to the next generation. Native Americans today carry on many of those ancient traditions.

Today, there are over 600 groups of Native Americans in Canada. Like other cultures around the world, the cultures of Native Americans were shaped by the forces of the environments in which they lived. In this section you will read about the major culture groups in Canada.

Culture Regions

Scientists have organized the Native Americans of Canada into six major culture regions. These regions are the Arctic, Subarctic, Eastern Woodlands, Great Plains, Plateau, and Northwest Pacific Coast.

Arctic As you read earlier, the Arctic is a harsh region inhabited by the Inuit. You may know the Inuit by another name—Eskimo. The Inuit were given the name Eskimo by the Cree. Eskimo means "eaters of raw meat." However, the Inuit do not eat raw meat. Inuit is the name this group calls itself. Inuit means simply "the people."

As you have read, the Inuit of the Northwest Territories signed an agreement with the Canadian government giving the Inuit control over a new territory called Nunavut. The Inuit tried for over 15 years to reach this agreement. The agreement is one of the largest peaceful land transfer deals in history. In return for gaining Nunavut, however, the Inuit had to give up their claim to another 640,000 square miles (1.7 million sq. km) of traditional lands. These lands may contain gas and oil fields.

Subarctic The Subarctic region is located just south of the Arctic. It is the largest region of Canada, stretching from the Atlantic coast in the east to the mountain ranges in the west. Major groups in the eastern portion of the region include the Cree and the Naskapi. In the west, live the Kutchin, Carrier, Dogrib, and Chipewyan, among other groups.

Traditionally, the people of the Subarctic were nomads. They moved from place to place following herds of animals. The subarctic people also relied on fish from the lakes and rivers of the region. The poor soil and harsh climate of the Subarctic made farming impossible. Today, many subarctic people live in settled villages. A number, however, still hunt and fish for a living.

Eastern Woodlands The people of the Eastern Woodlands lived in the lowlands of the St. Lawrence–Great Lakes region and the southern Maritimes. The woodlands were home to many groups including the Huron, Iroquois, Ojibwa, and Micmac. Because of the mild climate and good soil, many of the groups in this region lived in settled villages and farmed the land.

Great Plains Years ago, great herds of bison, sometimes called buffalo, roamed the plains of North America. In the southern portions of Manitoba, Saskatchewan, and Alberta, the Blackfoot and the Plains Cree followed the buffalo. They ate the meat of the animal, used the hide for clothing, and the bones for tools. When white settlers came to the Great Plains, they nearly drove the buffalo to extinction, or total destruction. The decline of the buffalo drastically changed the Plains Native American way of life.

Plateau The Plateau is a small region in the southeast portion of British Columbia. In the grassy valleys, such groups as the Okanogan, Colville, and Lake fished, hunted, and traded with the Native Americans who lived on the plains and Pacific coast.

Pacific Northwest The mild climate of the Pacific coast of Canada allowed such peoples as the Bellacolla, Wakashan, and Mootka to live in settled villages year round. They caught salmon in the rivers and hunted whale in the ocean waters.

Europeans Arrive

The first contact between Native Americans and Europeans occurred about the year 1000. Vikings from Scandinavia sailed west from Greenland and landed on the coast of Newfoundland. The Vikings tried to establish a settlement, but Native Americans drove them away.

About five hundred years later, Europeans again sailed into the North Atlantic waters. They made contact with Native Americans living along the coast. This time, the Native Americans were friendly. The Europeans began to fish the waters and to trade beaver skins with the Native Americans.

The Fur Trade The trade in beaver skins had a huge impact on Native American life. Felt hats made from beaver skin were in fashion among European men during the 1500s. European traders could make fortunes in the fur trade. Native Americans were eager to trade the fur for metal tools, guns, and other goods from Europe.

Canada's diverse Native Americans are determined to preserve their individual ways. Above, at a gathering of Cayuga Iroquois, old ways are celebrated.

Over the next hundred years, Native Americans trapped beaver in greater and greater numbers. At the same time, French settlers began to establish permanent colonies along the St. Lawrence River. The French founded Quebec in 1608 and Montreal in 1642.

Eager to profit from the fur trade, the English set up trading posts around the Hudson Bay area. The French and English competed for control of the fur trade. Native Americans were able to take advantage of the conflict between the French and English to strike good deals for their fur. The Native American traders would get the English and French to bid against one another for the furs.

Eventually, competition between the French and English led to war. In 1763, the British defeated the French and took control of Canada. Many French, however, remained.

Missionaries Soon after the Europeans arrived in Canada, missionaries came to convert Native Americans to Christianity. French and English missionaries worked in much the same way as the Spanish missionaries you read about in Chapter 3.

Many Native Americans converted to Christianity. However, a number of those that did convert continued to practice the traditional ceremonies of their own cultures. They did not see a reason to choose between their traditional religions and their new religion — Christianity.

The missionaries, however, felt otherwise. As the number of Europeans in Canada increased, missionaries did all they could to force Native Americans to give up their cul-

Each spring, Native Americans brought fur pelts to French trading posts. The trade brought wealth to Native Americans, but it changed their lives forever.

tures. Children were sent to missionary schools where they were punished for speaking their native languages. They learned French or English and dressed in European styles. Made to give up their native cultures, the children were taught to think and act like Europeans.

Disease: A Fatal Blow Perhaps the worst blow to Native Americans in Canada came in the form of disease. In much the same way as the Spanish and Portuguese exposed Native Americans in Latin America to disease, so did the French and English in Canada. Tens of thousands of Native Americans fell to diseases such as smallpox and measles. Native Americans had no immunity against these diseases. Whole communities disappeared in a matter of years.

Conflict Over Land The fur trade, missionaries, and disease took a terrible toll on Native American culture. As more Europeans arrived in the 1700s and 1800s, yet another threat to Native Americans emerged. Land-hungry settlers pushed Native Americans out of areas the settlers wished to own. Sometimes Native Americans were forced to sign treaties giving up their lands. In other cases, Native Americans fought openly to keep the land. However, whether they willingly signed treaties or went to war, the result was always the same — Native Americans were driven off their lands.

During the 1830s, the British began what they called a "civilization" program. They forced Native Americans to live on large tracts of land, called reserves. A similar program was being carried out in the United States, where the lands were called reservations.

Most often, the land on the reserve was divided among the Native Americans who were to live there. Each family received a plot of land to farm. But many Native American groups were nomads or hunters and gatherers. Farming was not part of their

Mohawks in Quebec march to protest the expansion of a golf course onto traditional land and to voice other grievances. The sign says "No to Racism."

In 1990, a group of Mohawk in Quebec protested the expansion of a golf course into traditional Mohawk territory. The Canadian government agreed to purchase the land for the Mohawk nation. The Mohawk, however, decided to use the incident to stage protests. They wanted to bring to the public's attention other grievances they held, such as Native Americans' right to self-government.

When the government ignored their protests, the Mohawks blocked a main bridge connecting Montreal with the shores of the St. Lawrence River. Other Native American groups throughout Canada staged protests in sympathy with the Mohawks. The situation turned increasingly violent. The Quebec government had to ask the federal government to send troops in to help stop the protests.

After 78 days of protest and negotiation, the Native Americans surrendered. Although the issue of self-government had not been resolved, the Mohawk nation had succeeded in bringing the issue to the forefront.

culture. In addition, the lands they were given were often worthless.

Despite the hardships, many Native Americans managed to preserve their traditional cultures. Today there are about 555,000 Native Americans and Inuit in Canada. They make up about 2 percent of the total population. Many groups are locked in battle with the Canadian government over land and cultural issues.

Fighting for Rights

As you read earlier, the Inuit managed to gain the territory of Nunavut from the Canadian government in the early 1990s. Other groups have waged similar fights.

Section 2 Review

1. List the six cultural regions scientists use to divide Canada's Native Americans. Choose two of the regions and describe how geography affects the Native American groups that live there.

2. **Expressing an Opinion** Why did the Mohawks continue their protests after the Canadian government agreed to stop the expansion of the golf course? What is your opinion of their actions?

The Power to Win:
The Cree of James Bay

It was 1972. Sixteen-year-old Matthew Coon Come was graduating from high school when he read something that changed the course of his life. Coon Come remembers

> *I picked up a Montreal newspaper that had a map of what was then the new James Bay power project. I was stunned to see that my home, the place where I had played as a child, was going to be submerged [placed under water] under a gigantic lake.*

The Cree

Matthew Coon Come, a Cree Native American, lives in the James Bay region. The Cree have lived on lands around James Bay in northern Quebec for about 6,000 years. When Europeans arrived in Canada, the Cree were one of many Native American groups that took part in the fur trade. The Cree felt the effects of contact with the Europeans in the same ways that other Native American groups felt them. Cree children attended missionary schools and a number of Cree converted to Christianity. Many Cree died from European diseases.

The Cree, however, lived in an isolated area of Quebec. Once the fur trade declined, the people of Canada left the Cree pretty much on their own. The Canadian government did insist upon sending Cree children to distant boarding schools. Coon Come remembers the day when he was six years old and a Canadian official arrived by floatplane. The official was the first white person the boy had ever seen. He had come to remind Coon Come's father that it was time to send his son to boarding school.

James Bay I

In 1971, Coon Come was away from home finishing high school. That year, the Canadian government announced that the national utility company, Hydro-Quebec, would start "the project of the century." The project, known as James Bay I, aimed to harness the power of the rivers in the James Bay region. To do this, Hydro-Quebec would construct a huge dam across the La Grand River. Hydro-Quebec would then build hydroelectric generating stations along the river's rapids. **Hydroelectricity** is power that is produced by flowing water. The electricity created by the power plants would be transmitted hundreds of miles south to Montreal and to cities in the

A Cree father and son prepare for a journey on the La Grand River in northern Quebec. The James Bay dam has endangered the traditional Cree way of life.

United States. It was an ambitious project that would create jobs and income for the province of Quebec.

Yet, damming the La Grand would flood thousands of acres of ancient Cree hunting and burial grounds. The government of Quebec did not even bother to tell the Cree and Inuit who lived in the area about the project. They heard about it through radio reports. The Cree and Inuit banded together to fight the project, but their efforts failed. Hydro-Quebec was allowed to build the dam and power stations.

After the dam was built, about 4,425 square miles (11,400 sq. km) of Cree and Inuit territory lay under water. The area under water is as large as the state of Connecticut. The flooding created terrible problems for the Cree. Fish, a main part of the Cree diet, became contaminated as a result of mercury poisoning. Caribou, beavers, and many birds lost their feeding grounds and homes. The flow of rivers and the cycle of floods changed. The environment of the James Bay region was thrown out of balance.

In addition, Hydro-Quebec built roads to bring supplies and equipment to construct the dam and electric plants. This opened a once-isolated region to sport hunters, loggers, mining companies, and others. Outsiders brought rapid change to Cree villages. Not all the changes were good. For example, before the influx of outsiders, Cree society was practically free from drug and alcohol abuse, divorce, and suicide. Suddenly the Cree faced these and other problems.

After James Bay I was well underway, the Cree and Inuit signed the James Bay and Northern Quebec Agreement (1975) with Canada. The pact granted the Cree approximately $135 million to compensate for lost land, exclusive hunting and fishing rights to 29,000 square miles (75,000 sq. km) of land, and the right to have a say in future projects.

Broken Promises: James Bay II

After signing the James Bay and Northern Quebec Agreement, the Cree felt safe from further threats to their land. But then in the late 1980s, Hydro-Quebec announced plans to build roads into Cree lands and construct additional dams and power plants. The Cree were outraged. By this time Matthew Coon Come had risen to become Grand Chief of the Quebec Cree. He and others led the fight against Hydro-Quebec.

First, the Cree and Inuit took Hydro-Quebec to court to block them from building roads. Then, in April 1990, a group of Cree and Inuit paddled a boat from Hudson Bay south. They traveled on the Hudson River all the way to New York City. They hoped to make their case public by bringing it to the attention of the people of the United States, especially New Yorkers. New York was thinking about buying power from Hydro-Quebec's James Bay project. In 1992, New York State canceled its plans to buy power. In addition, many in Quebec began to believe that the energy project was too costly. Considering the damage to the environment, they wondered whether the project was really worthwhile after all. Two years later, in November 1994, Hydro-Quebec put James Bay II on "indefinite hold." For the time being, the project was stopped.

Coon Come and the Cree vow never to stop fighting plans to destroy their land. "Everything flows from the land," says Coon Come. "As long as we have it, the Cree will survive."

Case Study Review

1. What is James Bay I and how did it affect life for the Cree and Inuit in the region?

2. **Analyzing Cause and Effect** How did the building of roads and dams cause the life of the Cree to change?

The People of Canada Today

Why is Canada called "a small nation in a big country"?

Though Canada is a land of great wealth, there is one natural resource in short supply — people. Canada is far larger in area than the United States. Yet it has only about one tenth the people. This has led some people to describe Canada as "a small nation in a big country."

Canada's people are not spread out evenly over its vast territory. If they were, they would be very isolated from one another. About 85 percent of all Canadians live within 200 miles (334 km) of the U.S. border. Most of Canada's large cities are located close to the U.S. border.

Divided by Language

Canada has two official languages, English and French. If you travel in Canada, you will see road signs in both languages.

One of Canada's biggest challenges is the disagreement between English-speaking Canadians and French Canadians. Almost one third of Canada's people speak French as a first language. The province of Quebec is about 85 percent French Canadian. Many of the people of Quebec consider themselves citizens of Quebec first and of Canada second.

People of British background make up about 40 percent of Canada's population. Many are descended from people who came from Ireland, England, and Scotland. Others are descendants of people who left the United States after the American Revolution. Descendants are people who can trace their heritage back to an individual or a group.

The rivalry between English speakers and French speakers is well known. This causes people to think that these are the only two culture groups in Canada. Actually, Canada has a great variety of people. As you have read, the first Canadians were Native Americans and Inuit.

In the past 100 years, people from all over Europe have come to settle in Canada. Many Canadians in western Canada have their roots in Asia. One way to understand Canadian culture is to look at its different provinces.

The Maritime Provinces

The eastern part of Canada has a long and rich history. The French were the first Europeans to settle in this region. They cleared the forests and worked the land in a colony called Acadia. France lost Acadia to Britain as a result of a war in 1713. However, few British came to settle there at first. People from Germany did come. Their descendants still live today in Nova Scotia.

In 1753, the British threw French settlers out of Acadia. British troops burned farms and arrested the Acadians. Then the Acadians were loaded on ships and sent to various British colonies.

Many of the French eventually came back to Acadia. But the best land had been taken. Today, there is a growing French Canadian population in the Maritime provinces.

The next wave of settlers to the Maritimes came from Scotland in the mid-1700s. Scots settlements grew in New Brunswick and Nova Scotia (which means "New Scotland" in Latin). Today, many people here have an accent like that of the Scots people.

A new wave of settlers arrived in the Maritime provinces with the beginning of the American Revolution. Colonists who had been loyal to the British left the American colonies. Many of them settled in the Maritimes.

Quebec

West of the Maritime provinces is the large province of Quebec. More than 85 percent of Quebec's people speak French. About

CANADA: ITS PROVINCES AND TERRITORIES

Facts About Canada

Capital City: Ottawa
Size (sq. mi.): 3,844,907
Population: 27,351,000
Population Density: 7.2 persons per square mile
Ethnic Groups: 40% British, 27% French, 20% Other Europeans, 2% Native Americans, 11% other (includes Americans, Russians, Ukrainians, Chinese, and Japanese)

The Provinces	Size (sq. mi.)	Population
Alberta	255,287	2,545,553
British Columbia	365,947	3,282,061
Manitoba	250,947	1,091,942
New Brunswick	28,355	723,900
Newfoundland	156,949	568,474
Nova Scotia	21,425	899,942
Ontario	412,581	10,084,885
Prince Edward Island	2,185	129,765
Quebec	594,860	6,895,963
Saskatchewan	251,866	988,928
The Territories		
Northwest Territories*	1,322,909	57,649
Yukon	186,661	27,797

Sources: *The World Almanac and Book of Facts 1994*; "Canada" *Microsoft Encarta '95.*

*In 1992, voters in the Northwest Territories approved the creation of Nunavut, a self-governing territory to be carved from the Northwest Territories. Nunavut will cover an area of about 772,000 square miles and have a population of 21,000 (mostly Inuit people). It is scheduled to begin in 1999.

Spread out over ten provinces and two territories, Canada is the world's second largest country. How many Canadian provinces have more than three million people?

two million French-speaking people of Quebec have moved to the United States. There they live mainly in New England and in New York State.

Quebec is a Native American word for "the place where the river narrows." At such a place along the St. Lawrence River, Samuel de Champlain (sham•PLAYN) established a French post in 1608. There French settlers cut down trees and built small buildings. The colonists cleared fields and planted wheat and other crops.

Quebec remained a colony of France until 1763. In that year, the French signed a treaty ending a long and bitter war with Britain. The British took over Canada.

However, British rule did not change the way the people of Quebec lived. They continued to speak French. They also practiced their Roman Catholic religion.

Until recently, Quebec was very much a rural province. Tidy farms sat along riverbanks. Many of these farms were owned by the same family for many generations.

This part of Quebec still exists. In the rural areas, life revolves around the farm and the close-knit family. However, many of the people of Quebec have moved to cities to seek work.

Montreal is the largest city of Quebec. It has many English-speaking residents. But Montreal is a French Canadian city. Its major churches attract thousands of pilgrims each year.

Montreal is an important banking, shipping, and industrial city. The main portion of the city runs up the slip of an extinct volcano.

Quebec City, the province's other major city, is the heart of French Canada. Quebec is a historic city. The "lower town" is tucked under the shadow of a high cliff. This is the site of the original French settlement of 1608.

To the north lies a vast treasure house of resources. Until recently, few people lived in northern Quebec. Mainly Cree, Inuit, and other native groups lived there in isolated villages. However, great mineral wealth has been discovered underneath the rocky Canadian Shield. As you have read in Case Study 7, huge hydroelectric plants have been built along Quebec's rushing rivers.

Ontario

Ontario is almost as big as Quebec. In many other ways, it is similar. Both Ontario and Quebec border on the United States. Both reach far up to the north. Both are heavily populated in the south and lightly populated in the north.

Yet Ontario and Quebec are different in one important way. Quebec is the center of French Canada. Ontario is British in language and culture.

English-speaking settlers in the late 1700s found the St. Lawrence valley already settled by French Canadians. Thus they traveled further west. Here they found a rich triangle of land that cut down to the Great Lakes. Many of these settlers were fleeing during the American Revolution.

Today, Ontario is one of Canada's fastest growing regions. It is also the most ethnically diverse province. Ontario's capital city, Toronto, boasts many ethnic neighborhoods. It also has radio and television stations that broadcast in over 20 foreign languages.

The Prairie Provinces

West from Ontario, the green eastern landscapes give way to the rolling "prairie provinces." These three provinces grow most of the wheat that makes Canada the fourth-largest wheat producer in the world.

Here in the prairies, it is clear that Canadians are not all of French and British origins. These provinces are almost as ethnically diverse as Ontario. Slightly less than half of the people of the prairies claim

In the provinces of Manitoba, Saskatchewan, and Alberta, the fertile land, summer rains, and dry harvest season make the prairies ideal for growing wheat. Canada is one of the world's largest producers of wheat.

Vancouver is one of the world's most beautiful cities. Locate the city on the map on page 85. How do you think Vancouver's location encourages trade with Asia?

British ancestry. Ethnic groups in the prairies include the descendants of eastern European immigrants who came to Canada around 1875.

The Métis are another group that live in the prairies. They are descendants of French trappers and Native American women who settled here more than 100 years ago. They settled in a cold, dry land that was supposed to be bad for farming. Through years of struggle, they created some of Canada's most successful farms.

The Pacific Coast

Look at the map of Canada on page 85. You will see that cities such as Vancouver and Victoria are quite far north. In fact, they are located north of Montreal, Minnesota, or Maine. Yet the climate is so gentle that flowers begin to bloom as early as February or March. That's because the Pacific coast benefits from warm ocean currents.

This mild climate is partly responsible for the rapid growth in population of Canada's Pacific coast region. Many people have moved there to find work in the new industries of the Pacific coast.

Vancouver is one of Canada's fastest-growing cities. Its harbor teems with activity. From the docks of Vancouver, Canadian products are shipped to Australia, Asia, and other parts of the world.

British Columbia has drawn people from all over the world. Asians are an important part of the population. The first Chinese Canadians came to the area more than 100 years ago. Many came to build the Canadian Pacific Railroad. This railroad was cut through the Rockies to connect western Canada with the prairies.

People from Japan and India followed. In recent years, a large number of people have come from parts of East and Southeast Asia. A large number of Chinese have come from Hong Kong. These new immigrants are usually well educated and wealthy.

Section 3 Review

1. How have French Canadians maintained their culture?
2. **Drawing Conclusions** Do you think calling Canada "a small nation in a big country" is accurate? Why or why not?

Changing Patterns of Life

Why do many French Canadians want to declare Quebec independent from Canada?

Though Canadians live in thousands of scattered villages, Canada is an urban country. At the beginning of the 1900s, less than 40 percent of all Canadians lived in cities. Now, close to 80 percent do. One main reason for this shift is the growth of industry in the cities.

About three out of ten Canadians live in Canada's three largest cities, Toronto, Montreal, and Vancouver. Toronto is now the nation's center for industry and finance. Montreal is the world's second largest French-speaking city. Vancouver handles most of Canada's exports to the nations of Asia.

The Changing Face of Canada

Most Canadians are either of British or French origin. However, about one third are neither. Canada has brought together a variety of people. In Toronto, Canadians from Jamaica play cricket on Sundays. Chinese Canadians in Vancouver celebrate the Chinese New Year with dragon dances. Ukrainian Canadians decorate brightly colored Easter eggs. German Canadians on the prairies celebrate the harvest with an "Oktoberfest."

In many ways, Canadians are still trying to complete their mosaic. They have all the

Canadians take great pride in their country and its ethnic heritage. They celebrate their diversity at festivals such as this summertime meeting in Quebec.

independent pieces. However, they are trying to fit these pieces into an overall picture of Canada.

The French Canadian Challenge

Almost all of the "new Canadians" have adopted the English language. This has helped make French Canadians feel isolated. In all provinces but Quebec, they feel shut out of the mainstream. This has led them to resent other Canadians.

The reasons for this resentment can be traced far back into Canada's history. As you have read, the British and French fought for control of Canada in the 1700s. After the British won control, the government, society, and culture of Canada took on a British character. In recent years, Canadians have tried to narrow the differences between English- and French-speaking Canadians. Language is one issue. Many of the French speakers resent the dominance of English. Economic control is another issue. The French speakers resent that the English speakers often hold the best-paying jobs.

The Canadian government has tried to protect the French language. One result is **bilingualism,** the use of two languages.

On Assignment. . .

What would you tell visitors to Canada about its many cultures? Which cities would you recommend that tourists visit? Why?

French and English are both official languages of Canada. Signs and government papers are printed in English and French. At official ceremonies, Canada's national anthem is always sung in English and in French.

Separatism

Since 1960, French speakers have taken over much of the economic life in Quebec. Yet many French Canadians are not satisfied by these changes. They are concerned that their culture will be overshadowed by the culture of English-speaking Canada.

"Long live free Quebec!" is the slogan of the French Canadian separatists. Separatists want Quebec to be independent from the rest of Canada. In 1995, the voters of Quebec came within a hair of voting to leave Canada. By a margin of less than 1 percent, voters in Quebec chose to remain a province of Canada. However, the debate over Quebec remains. Some people think it is only a matter of time until Quebec wins its independence.

Many Canadians worry about the problems that an independent Quebec would create. It would split the country in two. Quebec separates the four Maritime provinces from the rest of Canada. Trade, transportation, and communications among those provinces would be difficult if Quebec were independent.

Canada and the United States

Armed with its rich resources, Canada has taken its place among the world's leaders. Canada belongs to several international organizations. Canadian troops have served in United Nations peace-keeping operations.

However, Canada's closest ties are with the United States. The two countries have long been friendly. More than two thirds of Canada's trade is with the United States. The United States is the main buyer of Canadian resources. American investors control a large portion of Canadian industry.

However, many Canadians are concerned about the strong influence of U.S. business and culture. Most popular magazines in Canada are U.S. magazines. U.S. television programs are shown over all of Canada. Popular music and fast foods also reflect the U.S. influence.

Despite these concerns, the United States and Canada are close allies for the most part. Sometimes the neighbors squabble. But the peace arch at the border between Washington State and British Columbia is a symbol of the friendship that exists between the two countries.

Canada and the World

Canada, like the United States, is a democracy. While it is an independent country, it has close ties with Britain.

Canada is a member of the **Commonwealth of Nations.** The commonwealth is made up of independent countries that were once part of the British Empire. Members of the commonwealth have agreements with one another. There are 47 members in all. Queen Elizabeth II of Britain heads the commonwealth. However, she does not govern any of the member countries.

The government of Canada is a **federal system.** The power to make laws is divided between the federal government in Ottawa and the governments of the ten provinces.

There has often been a tug-of-war between the federal and the provincial governments. Disputes have arisen over who controls natural resources. The powers of the provincial governments are another source of conflict.

Section 4 Review

1. Why have Canada's cities grown so large in recent years?

2. **Understanding Points of View** Why do many Canadians resent the influence of U.S. culture? What might they do to preserve their own culture?

I. Reviewing Vocabulary

Match each word on the left with the correct definition on the right.

1. mosaic
2. bilingualism
3. hydroelectric
4. federal system

a. design made up of many small pieces
b. a system in which government power is divided between a central government and a local government
c. power that comes from the force of rushing water
d. the policy of recognizing two official languages

II. Understanding the Chapter

Answer the questions below on a separate sheet of paper.

1. In what region of Canada are most of its lakes?
2. How are the provinces of Quebec and Ontario similar? different?
3. What three provinces make up the region known as "Canada's breadbasket"? How did these provinces earn that name?
4. Why do French Canadians resent the culture of English Canada?

III. Building Skills: Studying a Map

Study the map on page 85. Answer the following questions on another sheet of paper.

1. Which province or territory of Canada is located farthest east? Which is located farthest west?
2. Which city is the capital of Canada?
3. What oceans border Canada?

IV. Working Together

Work with several classmates to construct a debate about independence for Quebec. Half your group will argue for independence and half will argue against it. Use information in this chapter to build your arguments. Hold your debate in class.

On Assignment. . .

Making a Presentation: Review the notes you took while reading the chapter. Remember that your audience is people who will be visiting Canada. You may choose one of the following topics or come up with one of your own. One possible topic is how the landscape has prevented Canadian unity. The other topic is what a visitor to Toronto should know about the city. After you have made your choice, create an outline for your presentation. Then, write a narrative based on your outline and present it to the class.

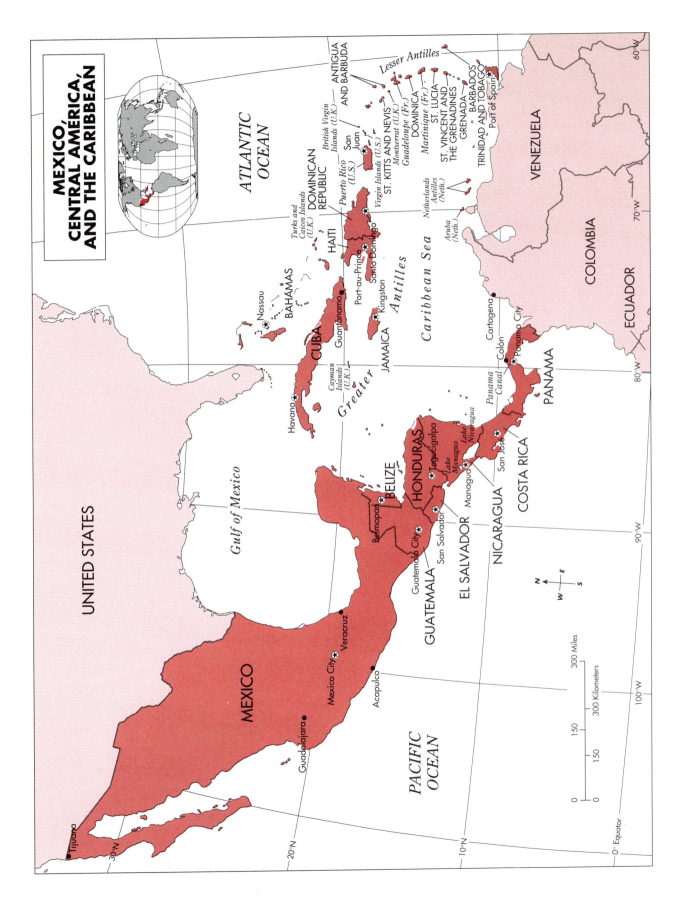

Map of Mexico, Central America, and the Caribbean

Caribbean Sea

ATLANTIC OCEAN

Caracas

VENEZUELA

GUYANA

SURINAME

10°N

Georgetown

French Guiana (Fr.)

Bogotá

Paramaribo

Cayenne

COLOMBIA

0° Equator

Quito

ECUADOR

Galapagos Is. (Ec.)

BRAZIL

Recife

PERU

Lima

10°S

La Paz

Brasília

BOLIVIA

Sucre

20°S

PARAGUAY

Rio de Janeiro

Tropic of Capricorn

São Paulo

ATLANTIC OCEAN

CHILE

30°S

Santiago

Buenos Aires

URUGUAY

Montevideo

ARGENTINA

PACIFIC OCEAN

N
W · E
S

SOUTH AMERICA

40°S

| 0 | 300 | 600 Miles |
| 0 | 300 | 600 Kilometers |

Falkland Is. (U.K.)

50°S

100°W   90°W   80°W   70°W   60°W   50°W   40°W   30°W   20°W

Map of South America

aqueduct (AK•wuh•dukt)   a system of pipes that carry water to where it is needed

bilingualism   the policy of recognizing two official languages

caudillo (kaw•DEE•yoh) a Spanish term for a military strongman

causeway   a raised road across water or marshland

chaperon (SHAP•uh•rohn)   an older person who goes with a boy and girl on a date to assure proper behavior

civilian   a citizen who does not belong to the military

commonwealth   a self-governing state with close ties to another more powerful state

Commonwealth of Nations   the group of nations that were once colonies of Great Britain

Creole   a person in Spanish Latin America whose parents or ancestors were Spanish

cultural diffusion   the spread of new ideas and new ways of doing things from one society to others

cultural diversity   many different cultures

culture   the way of life of a group of people, including their ideas, customs, skills, and arts

dialect   a form of a language that belongs to a certain region

drought   a long period without rain

exile   a person who lives in another country usually because of political disagreements

extended family   the family unit in most traditional societies, consisting of three or four generations living in one household

extract   to remove or take from

federal system   a system in which power is divided between a central government and a local government

glacier (GLAY•shuhr)   a huge sheet of ice

global village   a term that refers to the entire modern world in which diverse people communicate, share experiences, and depend on one another for resources

gunboat diplomacy   a foreign policy that calls for threatening the use of military force to achieve a country's goals

hydroelectricity   power that comes from the force of rushing water

illiterate   unable to read or write

immune   protected against a specific disease

interdependent   the state of being dependent on one another for support or survival

irrigation   a system of human-made ditches that carry water

land reform   a government policy that involves breaking up large estates and giving the land to peasants

liberation theology a belief that the Roman Catholic Church should take an active role in ending poverty in Latin America

mestizos people who are part Native American and part European

Middle Passage the journey across the Atlantic Ocean from West Africa to the Americas that was the route of the African American slave trade

mission a religious settlement devoted to spreading Christianity

moderate mild

mosaic a design made up of many small pieces of materials

mural a very large painting or photograph that is applied to a wall or ceiling

nomads people who have no permanent home but move from place to place in search of food and water

nuclear family the family unit in most developed societies, consisting often of a father, mother, and children

peninsula a body of land that is surrounded on three sides by water

peon a poor person who works all his or her life for rich landowners

province a territory governed as an administrative or political unit of a country

pyramid a building that is rectangular at its base with four triangular sides that meet at the top in a point

squatter person who settles on land he or she doesn't own

tariff a tax on goods entering or leaving a country

tropics lands that are near the equator

urban characteristic of a city or city life

viceroy a person who governs a colony as a representative of the king or queen

volcano a mountain with an opening near the top from which hot melted rocks, ash, and gases sometimes flow

INDEX

Acadia, 94
Africans in Latin America, 15, 16
Altitude, 19
Amazon River, 10, 11, 13, 18
America, first peoples of, 24, 87
Andes Mountains, 10, 11, 13, 18, 20, 28, 40
Aqueducts, 27
Arctic, 85, 87
Argentina, 11, 15, 16, 41, 43-44, 51, 52, 58, 61, 63
Arias, Oscar, 64
Art, 76-77
Aymará, 19, 20-21
Aztecs, 24, 26-27, 29-32

Batista, Fulgencio, 66
Beliefs and customs, as element of culture, 3
Bilingualism, 99
Bolívar, Simón, 40-41
Bolivia, 11, 16, 21, 28, 51-52, 59, 61
Brazil, 10, 15, 16, 17, 30, 51, 58, 61
  farming in, 19
  independence of, 42
  land reform in, 59-60
  under Portugal, 37
Britain, 83, 89, 94, 95, 98, 99
British Columbia, 97
Buffalo, 88

Cacao, 19
Canada, 82-99
  climate of, 86
  cultures of, 94-97, 98
  government of, 99
  international relations of, 99
  languages of, 94, 98-99
  Native Americans of, 87-93, 94, 97
  natural resources of, 86, 96
  Quebec separatism in, 99
  regions of, 83-85
Canadian Pacific Railroad, 97
Canadian Shield, 84, 96
Caracas, Venezuela, 54-55

Caribbean islands, 10, 12, 15, 35
Castro, Fidel, 59, 66-67
Cattle, 11, 19
Caudillos, 63
Causeways, 27
Central America, 12, 63-64, 65,
  See also specific countries
Central Plains, 84-85
Chamorro, Violeta Barrios de, 64-65
Champlain, Samuel de, 95
Chaperon, 50
Chile, 16, 28, 41, 44, 52, 61
Chinese Canadians, 97, 98
Cities and towns, Canadian, 95-96, 97, 98
Cities and towns, Latin American, 10, 51-55, 58, 59-60
  of early civilizations, 24, 25, 26, 27, 28
  mega-cities, 52
  slums, 51, 52, 54-55, 60
  Spanish colonial, 36
Civilian government, 63
Climate, 6
  in Canada, 86
  in Latin America, 10, 12-14, 19
Coffee, 19, 61
Colombia, 11, 19, 40, 41, 63
Columbus, Christopher, 29
Commonwealth, 71
Commonwealth of Nations, 99
Constitutional monarchy, 5
Constitutions, 43, 63
Cortés, Hernán, 29, 30, 31
Costa Rica, 64
Cree, 87, 91-93, 96
Creoles, 36-37, 40, 41
Cuauhtémoc, 32
Cuba, 15, 16, 17, 44, 59, 61, 66-67, 72
Cultural diffusion, 5
Cultural diversity, 2, 47
Cultural features, 7
Culture, 2-8, 47-51

Debt crisis, 65
Democracy, 5, 63-64

Deserts, 13, 15, 18
Dialect, 48
Díaz, Porfirio, 42-43
Dictatorship, 5, 42-43
Diseases, European, 31, 89
Dominican Republic, 17

Eastern Woodlands, 87
Economic growth, in Latin America, 65
Economic system, 4-5
Ecuador, 19, 28, 41
El Morro, 71
El Salvador, 64
Equator, 13
Eskimo, 87
Europeans in Latin America, 15, 16, 17, 44
Exiles, 58
Explorers, 29
Extended family, 3-4, 49-50

Family
  Aymará, 21
  extended, 3-4, 49-50
  nuclear, 3, 4
Farming
  crops, 19, 61
  development of, 24
  of Incas, 28
  land ownership and, 53
  Native American, 18, 20-21
  Spanish colonial, 37
Federal system, 99
Foods, of Latin America, 50-51
Foreign investment, 44
France, 39, 42, 89, 94, 95, 98, 99
Free enterprise systems, 4-5
French Canadians, 94, 95-96, 98-99
Fur trade, 88-89

Garcia Márquez, Gabriel, 77
Gauchos, 43
Geography, themes of, 6-8
Glaciers, 24

ACKNOWLEDGMENTS

Grateful acknowledgment is made to the following for illustrations, photographs, and reproductions on the pages indicated.

Photo credits: **p. 1:** Ron Chapple/FPG; **p. 3**: Sean Sprague/Impact Visuals; **p. 4:** Courtesy of the United Nations; **p. 7:** Sid Lathan/Photo Researchers; **p. 9:** Donna DeCesare/Impact Visuals; **p. 11:** the United Nations; **p. 11:** Daniel Aubrey/Odyssey/Chicago; **p. 11:** Robert McCollum; **p. 15:** Heraldo and Flavia de Faria Castro/FPG; **p. 16:** Harvey Finkle/Impact Visuals; **p. 16:** Sean Sprague/Impact Visuals; **p. 16:** Antonina Giammanco; **p. 17:** Robert McCollum; **p. 18:** Heraldo Castro/FPG; **p. 19:** Robert Frerck/Odyssey; **p. 23:** Robert Frerck/Odyssey **p. 25:** Robert Frerck/Odyssey; **p. 27:** Madrid-Bibliotheque Nationale; **p. 28:** Courtesy of the Canadian Pacific Railroad; **p. 30:** Madrid-Bibliotheque Nationale/Laurie Platt Winfrey; **p. 31:** The Granger Collection; **p. 34:** Karen Reinhard/FPG; **p. 35:** The Schomburg Center for Research in Black Culture; **p. 36:** Museo de America, Madrid, "Veracruz"; **p. 38:** Laurie Platt Winfrey, Inc./Carousel; **p. 39:** Library of Congress; **p. 40:** New York Public Library; **p. 43:** Robert Frerck/Odyssey; **p. 46:** Robert Frerck/Odyssey; **p. 48:** Robert Frerck/Odyssey; **p. 50:** Robert Frerck/Odyssey; **p. 53:** Robert Frerck/Odyssey; **p. 54:** John Bunting/Impact Visuals; **p. 57:** Eduardo Garcia/FPG; **p. 59:** Robert Frerck/Odyssey; **p. 60:** Telegraph Colour Library/FPG; **p. 61:** Courtesy of the United Nations; **p. 63:** Robert Frerck/Odyssey; **p. 64:** Harriet Harshorn/Impact Visuals; **p. 65:** Donna De Cesare/Impact Visuals; **p. 70:** © Travel Pix/FPG; **p. 72:** Library of Congress; **p. 73:** Robert Frerck/Odyssey; **p. 76:** Ricardo Funari/Impact Visuals; **p. 77:** Robert Frerck/Odyssey; **p. 79:** UPI/Bettmann; **p. 82:** James Blank/FPG; **84:** Robert Frerck/Odyssey; **p. 86:** Earl Roberge/Photo Researchers; **p. 87:** John Eastcott/YVA Momatiuk/Photo Researchers; **p. 88:** David Blumenfeld/Impact Visuals; **p. 89:** The Granger Collection; **p. 90:** Jim West/Impact Visuals; **p. 92:** Kirk Condyles/Impact Visuals; **p. 96:** Renaud Thomas/FPG; **p. 97:** Porterfield/Chickering, Photo Researchers; **p. 98:** Ferrell Graham, Photo Researchers.